SIM[ ]
ANXIOUS

Notes on
Anxiety Recovery

Lisa Towers
@simply_anxious

Copyright © 2022 Lisa Towers

DISCLAIMER

The purpose of this book is to educate, inspire, and motivate the reader. It is not advice on the subject matter covered. This book should not be used to diagnose or treat any medical conditions. Always consult your doctor for diagnosis or treatment. The author does not assume any responsibility for errors, omissions, or other interpretations of the subject matter. The purchaser or reader of this book assumes full responsibility of the use of this material and information. This book is for information only and should not be used to self-diagnose or replace professional help.

DEDICATION

To my mum and dad who kept me safe, and always encouraged me to carry on.

Thank you both for supporting and loving me through my life and being my rock through my darkest times.

I love you x

CONTENTS

Introduction 6

Chapter One: My Story 8

Chapter Two: The Things I Had to Change If I Were Ever to Recover 20

Chapter Three: You Are Not Broken, Damaged or Crazy 32

Chapter Four: What Anxiety Is and What It Isn't 39

Chapter Five: Anxiety Symptoms...........................45

Chapter Six: Anxiety Recovery and What I Learned 56

Chapter Seven: Soothing and Grounding Techniques That Helped Me Cope with Anxiety 79

Chapter Eight: My Hero, Dr Claire Weekes 87

Chapter Nine: My Experience with Medication 92

Chapter Ten: The Power of Being Patient 97

Chapter Eleven: Posts From My @SIMPLY_ANXIOUS Instagram Page...100

Chapter Twelve: Resources That Helped with My Recovery 152

Introduction

Anxiety is a widespread yet treatable mental health condition. But often (due to long waiting lists to see an NHS therapist and because not everyone can afford a private therapist) people end up suffering for longer than necessary. As a result, people are often left feeling incredibly isolated and lost. For this very reason I decided to write this book to share my own journey with recovery in the hope that it encourages others with their own recovery and helps them to feel less alone.

If you are struggling with anxiety and feeling stuck, then this book may be exactly what you need to inspire you to work on your recovery. For years, I've wanted to write something about my experience with anxiety and how I finally recovered. I am not a therapist or a medical professional, but I am someone who battled with anxiety for close to 20 years and finally worked through what sometimes feels like an impossible task to break free from the clutches of an anxiety disorder.

I've experienced the isolation, confusion, and frustration that anxiety can cause, and, through sheer desperation, I allowed myself to get scammed by the so-called anxiety experts, gurus, and other kinds of 'cure promises' over the years. Of course, I lost so much through suffering from anxiety: friends, relationships, job opportunities, holidays, to name a few of the things. But I also gained a lot of knowledge about anxiety: how the mind works, emotional wellbeing, life, and what's important. And I know without a shadow of a doubt that having better mental health and supporting your emotional wellbeing is essential to being able to lead a happier or more fulfilled life.

This book is a collection of my experiences, bite-sized information that helped me, and some of the most popular posts from my Instagram page, @simply_anxious. I hope it becomes a comfort for you to have this book when you need support, validation, or insight. It's a book I wish I'd had access to when suffering and going through my own recovery. And with that in mind, I'm hoping that it helps you to believe in yourself, acknowledge just how strong you are, and of course assists you on your recovery journey.

CHAPTER ONE

My Story

Why I Created @simply_anxious

For years I wanted to share my experience of anxiety with a wider audience. I wanted to share what I had learnt, the valuable stuff, the lightbulb moments, and (of course) the not-so-valuable stuff. I had learnt so much it would be a shame to keep it to myself and not use it in a way that could possibly help others. I wanted to prevent others from suffering for as long as I did, or for those who had, to see why it is never too late to move through anxiety and recover.

Anxiety feels extremely isolating and scary, and can leave you believing there is something seriously wrong with you. But that is not true, and my @simply_anxious page explains why.

I wanted my page to lead people to a place of confidence and peace, and (more importantly) a new and healthier relationship with anxiety. I wanted anyone who was still looking for that magic pill, wasting time and money on miracle cures, to stop searching. I wanted people to see that they have everything they need to recover right there inside of themselves.

My @simply_anxious page is written with love and honesty, and everything I share I've experienced, learnt, or discovered for myself.

I spent years believing there was a certain type of person who suffered from anxiety, and that was me. If asked to describe what an anxious person's traits were, I would have said 'me'. I thought I was the 'type' because becoming ill with anxiety had happened to me and I didn't know anyone else who suffered. One thing that became apparent when I started raising awareness on mental health was how the stigma attached to mental health conceals just how common anxiety is and how anyone can develop an anxiety disorder. The truth is that anxiety doesn't discriminate and is one of the most common mental health conditions globally. So if you think you're weak or damaged or alone, you're wrong!

I have heard so many stories from men and women from all walks of life describing the sheer terror they experienced while suffering from anxiety and/or panic. I saw how anxiety doesn't favour a particular gender, geographical location, or age group. It can and does affect anyone. I also found that the reasons people find themselves suffering can differ. I met people who told me theirs started from past trauma, emotional and mental stress, illness, financial loss, and grief. Others told me that they began experiencing extreme mental exhaustion while studying at university. So my belief that anxiety was a sign that you're damaged, broken, or weak soon vanished.

Because of the stigma, we tend to put on a brave face around friends and family, meaning suffering goes unnoticed by the outside world. But, unfortunately, speaking first-hand here, this only fuels the anxiety, deepens the problem, and eventually leads to burnout or a complete mental breakdown. I often wonder how many people are still actually living like this today. Even with the amount of awareness coming to the forefront, I bet there are thousands, if not millions still out there suffering in silence, which breaks my heart.

I know how exhausting it is to carry on with life as if all is well when you feel like you're dying inside. I did it for years, using various ways to suppress and hide the truth. I felt utterly isolated and full of shame because I hadn't spoken openly to anyone outside of my family about my diagnosis, and, as I said earlier, I certainly didn't know of anyone else who suffered.

Everything began to change for me when I discovered how many others were struggling with anxiety via the internet. I befriended a small group of women from all over the world who also felt isolated in their struggle and were looking for some validation (we had joined up via a forum for a popular anxiety book and decided to set up our little group separately). By opening and sharing our stories, we began to learn more about anxiety, discover that recovery is possible, and (most importantly) feel less alone. We supported and encouraged each other along the way, which opened doors to some of us meeting in person, doing Secret Santas, and having Skype calls, which helped no end with our recoveries. Having other people to share my experience with and who understood what I was going through brought comfort and stopped the feeling of being alone.

@simply_anxious was created from my experience with this group of women and my voluntary work in campaigning to raise awareness and help break the stigma around mental health. Both showed me the value of sharing, talking, and connecting with others, and how empowering it can be for recovery. I wanted to share my story and create a community so others could feel seen, heard, and validated while they healed.

And this book is what naturally followed: to let you know that suffering from anxiety is not something you should feel ashamed of, hide away because of, or beat yourself up over. It is also not something that has to impact your life as negatively as it may be doing now. It is extremely common, and as you have hopefully noticed over the past few years, more people in the public eye are coming forward to share their experiences in the hope that mental health is finally accepted and treated in parity with physical health.

Please believe me when I say: you're not alone.

Why Did I Start Raising Awareness? What Happened After I Did?

The truth is I don't really know why other than I had become so tired of hiding the fact that I was suffering from an anxiety disorder like some dirty little secret. The more I learnt about anxiety, the more I realised that it wasn't my fault, it couldn't be just me who suffered at work, and by hiding it, I was making my experience worse.

I was at work (I worked for the UK government) participating in one of of the annual health and wellbeing events. I couldn't help but notice how they covered every topic except mental health. 'Why is that?' I kept thinking. It made me wonder how everyone else seems to cope. Then I remembered the online forum I had been using for a few months, which brought together women from across the globe. We used this group to chat about our struggles and support each other. So I knew I wasn't the only person suffering.

I wanted these kinds of conversations and support to be happening at work and not just online. So at the event, I sat next to a deputy director I knew pretty well and said to her, 'I wish they covered mental health topics at these events.' She responded, 'Really? Why is that?' and I just came out with it: 'Because I have been suffering with an anxiety disorder for decades and it is so isolating.' I paused for a second, thinking, 'Oh shit, this might have cost me my job,' when she replied, 'OMG, I've been suffering with depression, so I know exactly how you feel.'

That conversation changed everything. Soon after that, we created a staff support group called 'Break the Stigma'. We started running monthly lunchtime events to talk openly about our struggles and bring in guest speakers from places like The Samaritans, NHS, mindfulness experts, etc. The events were packed and would spill out into the corridor at times. We also started to receive more and more emails from staff across the UK who were suffering in silence and feeling isolated. Our mailing list soon grew into the hundreds.

It's funny how I struggled with social anxiety at the time but was able to stand in front of people talking about my own experience with anxiety. I can now see how my passion to be seen and heard to make a difference to others who were suffering gave me the courage to do it. I was most definitely on a mission, as was my colleague, and together we made a huge difference.

Break the Stigma became national, as we started assisting departments across the UK in setting up their groups in line with ours. We held awareness events across the UK, including one in 2014 at the head office in Whitehall, presenting to the heads of the Civil Service Disability and Diversity Board. At this presentation, we met Sue Baker – CEO of the national campaign 'It's Time to Change' – and we were invited to appear in their TV advertisement, broadcast across the UK at peak times. I couldn't believe how one conversation at a bog-standard annual health and wellbeing event had ended up with me on TV. And it didn't stop there.

We got invited to mental health VIP events with people like Deputy Prime Minister Nick Clegg, world champion boxer Frank Bruno, British journalist, TV broadcaster, and author Alistair Campbell, plus many more. Everyone was incredibly welcoming and kind. However, what struck me the most was how enthusiastic everyone was about doing everything they could to ensure mental health became viewed in parity with physical health. It filled me with joy to think that the stigma that kept people from getting the support they needed to heal was, at last, going to be addressed. It felt overwhelming after I'd been hiding my own anxiety for all those years, as you can imagine.

2014 – 2016 was without a doubt the time things started to change for mental health. But what I naïvely didn't realise back then was just how much work would still need to be done in 2022. The NHS needs more funds and to create more accessible treatments.

Back in 2016, Break the Stigma had introduced wellbeing rooms into government buildings instead of staff using the toilets when overwhelmed. We had some staff trained in mental health first aid and set up buddy support groups across the UK for the first time ever. We tried and did make a difference, and although not perfect, it was at least something to make life a little bit easier for those suffering from mental ill health in the workplace. However, the one issue that I couldn't see ever changing was the culture, and I am sorry to say I still believe it is the culture that is the leading cause of poor mental health in many working environments.

Raising awareness and trying to make a difference for mental health was something I loved doing. Even during the times when my anxiety was high, I somehow managed to dig deep and tell my story. As a result, I met so many wonderful like-minded people I am still in touch with today. To top it all, I was also awarded the British Empire Medal on the Queen's 2015 New Year Honours list for my contribution to mental health awareness.

The reason I have included this chapter is to show others that even though you may be struggling with anxiety, you are still capable of making a difference to things, especially if you can work outside of your comfort zone. I hadn't completely healed when I achieved all this: I actually had a big panic attack the day after I attended the Queen's Garden Party at Buckingham Palace. But what this experience did show me was how I could do hard things. It inspired me to use the same passion that I'd used to raise awareness about mental health for my own recovery. And that is exactly what I did.

My Anxiety Journey

Anxiety was something I suffered with on and off for 20 years. It shaped my life and became my identity. I was first diagnosed in the 1990s. Although my diagnosis was a shock it was also welcomed because it provided an explanation about what was happening to me. I was alarmed by the diagnosis because it was the first time I'd ever heard of the word 'anxiety', let alone understood the meaning of it. Never had I heard of anyone else suffering or anxiety being openly spoken about. I was 25 years old when I was diagnosed, so surely if it was a common illness then I would have heard about it before then?

Unfortunately, with the diagnosis came an incorrect prognosis that led me to believe I would suffer from anxiety for the rest of my life. My doctor tried to reassure me I'd be OK if I stayed on the medication and came to visit them once a month. I struggled terribly to understand why I was suddenly suffering from what I thought was an incurable illness. It was all very confusing as I had always been so independent and carefree. Yet here I was, back at my parents' home, unable to sleep or eat, and terrified of being in my own skin. So, naturally, this bred a lot of insecurities that I still struggle with today.

For a long time after that first diagnosis I believed I was 'damaged' and different from everyone else because, in the 1990s, nobody talked about anxiety, let alone suffered from it. It wasn't like today where you have the internet and social media where ordinary people like me as well as celebrities, sportspeople, and even royalty come forward to share their struggles with anxiety and panic attacks. Back then, it felt like a dirty little secret that only I had, and I needed to hide it for fear I'd be locked away and the key thrown away. It was undoubtedly a terrifying and lonely time for sure, which I wanted to prevent others from experiencing by writing this book and sharing my story.

The following nine to ten years were about coming to terms with my new life as an anxiety sufferer who needed daily medication and bi-weekly doctors/therapist appointments to keep sane, (well, that's what I thought at the time). Unfortunately, it was in those years I suffered in silence. Yes, my family knew, but that was all. I used alcohol to socialise and filled my time with yoga classes, learning the piano, and reading library books on mental health and anxiety. I would go overseas with my parents for the winter and have reiki, massages, and swimming to keep me calm and relatively anxiety-free. Those years were about me living as someone with a mental illness, as someone who would never recover (at this stage in my experience I had no idea that recovery was possible), and as someone wondering how the hell I'd got there.

As the years went by and the internet became more widespread, I began researching anxiety to try and learn more about my illness. It wasn't long before I came across adverts stating anxiety could be cured. This was a total shock as no one had ever told me that it was even a possibility to be cured or recover. However, I soon realised just how wrong my prognosis had been: that anxiety was, in fact, treatable, and you could go on to recover from it completely. Again, it was a total shock to find this out, but at the same time, I always sensed deep down that this 'thing' wasn't who I was. Now that recovery seemed obtainable, my appetite grew to learn more.

Unfortunately, because recovery was now an option, I became obsessed with it, and so I fell victim to every scam out there. I bought necklaces that promised to cure anxiety, bracelets that claimed they blocked anxiety, books on guaranteed methods that nearly broke the bank, and a ton of CDs that, if listened to six times a day, would fix you. But nothing worked. All these failed attempts to recover made me sink back into a pool of self-doubt that maybe my anxiety was the kind of anxiety that you couldn't recover from, and maybe my doctor had been right. These 'fixes' didn't work because, as this book goes on to explain, I didn't need 'fixing' or 'curing'. Nobody can overcome anxiety for you, and anxiety recovery is not a 'one-way suits all' thing you can buy off a website like teeth whitening kits. It's about unlearning, learning, facing, accepting, and growing through it all and reaching the other side of the fear.

But I didn't give up. I continued researching everything on the subject. The more I studied, the more empowered I became. I stumbled on Dr Claire Weekes's books, and later a book by Paul David, both of which inspired me and put me on the right path. They helped me to understand 'the WHYs', the symptoms, and the process needed to recover. I learnt how the fear response works, how adrenaline can produce distressing physical symptoms that are not harmful, and how you don't have to believe your thoughts. You can imagine the relief and comfort I got from all this validating and encouraging new information. I went from feeling damaged and unfixable to understanding everything I needed to know about anxiety and emotional/mental wellbeing, including how to overcome my fear of anxiety and by doing so break free from the anxiety disorder I was trapped in. I was now full of hope that I could recover and get my life back.

The knowledge I gained was the solid base I needed to work from in order to recover. It lifted me out of the depths of despair and inspired me to move forward gradually with my healing and, finally, a full recovery. And this is the reason I set up my @simply_anxious Instagram page and then wrote this book. I wanted to share as much as I could to inspire and support others not to give up hope and get their freedom back – just as I did. I hope that sharing everything I learnt about anxiety and recovery brings comfort and creates a solid base that reassures, empowers, and also motivates others to heal correctly.

CHAPTER TWO

The Things I Had to Change if I Were Ever to Recover

I Had to Stop Labelling Myself as Anxious

Something changed for me in 2016 while I was at an event to raise anxiety awareness. This realisation hit me so hard that it completely changed how I viewed anxiety forever.

I noticed how many people introduced themselves with their names and diagnosis during the event. 'Hi, I'm Lisa, an anxiety sufferer' or 'John here, I have bipolar and panic disorder'. It reminded me how I had been doing that very same thing. I had been wearing it like a badge of honour. But on this day, I could see how these beautiful, brave people had become lost in their diagnosis. Just like I had!!

I couldn't get that day out of my head: the realisation we'd all innocently taken on the role of sufferer. And when you label yourself as anything, that is what you will be because you tell yourself that is who you are! I kept thinking how disempowering this must be and recall looking over a sea of people and wondering how many of them were living as sufferers and forgetting all the good things about themselves. After that day, I began seeing my life differently: looking in a new direction; away from the victim I had become. I wanted to know who I was, what anxiety was, and uncover the self-limiting effect of this label.

Another thing I noticed was just how damaging my inner narrative had become because of this label. It was full of self-defeating negativity like: 'My Anxiety... I am Damaged... I am Anxious... I have a Mental Illness... I CAN'T do this... I SHOULD... I MUST.' No wonder I was constantly on high alert and unable to relax. I realised that somewhere amongst this mess, I had innocently given all my power away to ANXIETY and, by doing so, allowed it to run my life.

All this because when the anxiety first took hold of me, I had no idea what was happening. All because I believed what my doctor at the time had told me when he said I would have anxiety for the rest of my life and should just stay on the pills. Nobody told me I could recover or that what I was experiencing wasn't me and that my true self was still there underneath the chaos that my mind and nervous system were creating. If only I'd been told at the start that anxiety is something you experience, not something you are, it may have changed my whole ordeal.

So, what did I do to turn this around? Well, in short, first of all I stopped using the label and instead started referring to myself as someone who was recovering from chronic anxiety. When I stopped describing myself as 'anxious', I began to see that I was not damaged or doomed for life. Instead, I was healing and recovering, which took time. And this started to lighten the weight I'd been carrying.

By the way, this was by no means an instant fix, and it took me some time to change my beliefs about myself and anxiety. But this approach gently gave me my power back and helped the real me shine through.

Suffering from anxiety is horrendous, and it is something I wouldn't wish on anyone. Still, I believe that seeing it for what it is and not labelling yourself with it will allow you to heal much quicker. Look at it this way: if you label yourself as an anxious person who has panic attacks and can't do the things as other people can, you'll remain stuck in a very negative and self-limiting bubble.

But instead, try labelling yourself as a brilliant, intelligent, caring, and compassionate person (you can choose your own qualities: I'm sure there are many!) who is currently going through some emotional stuff and healing. That is (1) much kinder, and (2) a more accurate and authentic label to wear.

I'll end this section by saying that I also believe that carrying the 'I am an anxious person' label only prolonged my suffering and held me back in my recovery, and I don't want that to happen to you!

Other Changes I Had to Make

I found I had to make changes in both my lifestyle and behaviours to support my recovery process. So I thought it would be helpful to share those changes I made to aid my recovery and benefit my mental health. We are all different, so please don't take these as a 'must do' for yourself. They were just the things that I knew would help me recover correctly.

I had to be radically honest with myself here, and because it isn't always obvious what needs to change, I had to take a long hard look at myself to do it properly. (Journaling helped me with this.)

My career

Although being a civil servant is usually considered a job for life, the work culture and environment (competitive, toxic at times) had become a significant factor in my mental health decline. Although they claim to support staff who suffer from mental health conditions, it depends on the manager you have. There is no consistency in how people are treated, and while some get the encouragement and support they need, others are made to feel a burden. The latter was my experience: a senior manager feeling like a total burden. All because I had come up against a manager who had decided to make my life hell, and I tried to do something about it. I won't go into the detail of the specifics: the main point here is that because I couldn't ever see this kind of problem changing within that organisation, I had to consider how detrimental to my health it could be if I were to stay. So, after 20-odd years, I decided that leaving was the best option. I made the decision to go self-employed (supporting entrepreneurs streamline their business operations) while also training as a coach to help others. I understand leaving a job is a difficult option and not one to be made lightly, but it was the best decision I ever made. I have never looked back.

Alcohol consumption

Somewhere down the line, I developed the habit of using wine to cope with anxiety. It was the only alcoholic beverage I liked, and the one drink society saw as an acceptable drink to have after a bad day.

I think the rush of the feel-good hormone dopamine (your brain's 'reward centre') you get when you drink alcohol appealed to me as it acted as an instant relaxant and shut up those anxious thoughts that would trouble me throughout the day. Unfortunately, the alcohol buzz didn't last long, so I would end up drinking the whole bottle or more until I fell into bed. After that, it became my nightly routine. I also used wine before, during, and after any socialising.

The trouble is that the more you drink alcohol, the more you need to feel that dopamine rush and eventually serotonin (the 'happy chemical') becomes suppressed. That's why you feel anxious after drinking. Having a glass of wine or a beer to relax after a bad day may relax you in the short term, but as the alcohol leaves your body, anxiety returns with a vengeance, which made my suffering a million times worse.

I tried to stop this habit a few times by successfully doing the odd alcohol-free month here and there but always fell back into the same unhealthy pattern. So if I wanted to give myself a good chance of overcoming anxiety, I had to be true to myself and stop doing the things that were adding to it, and alcohol was one of them. So I made the decision to cut out alcohol until I felt that I had recovered.

It took a few tries, however, because the strange thing I find with alcohol is how easily it can creep back into your life. Even after you have had periods alcohol-free and felt the benefits like how alive you feel, how much more energy you have, how the brain fog that used to sit in your head for days no longer does, and how much better your hair and skin look. Even then, you can fall back into this unhealthy way of relaxing.

This is precisely what I did during Christmas of 2021. I started by having a few glasses of wine, and before I realised, I was back to buying a bottle a night which I drank at home alone. Then the fatigue, brain fog, daily sluggishness, and anxiety reappeared.

I had to admit that when it came to alcohol, I simply couldn't moderate. I was unable to have just one glass of wine and stop. And so, on 1st January 2022, I decided to quit for good because my mental health is way more important than a nightly bottle of Pinot Grigio. Several months later and I'm still alcohol-free. Alongside changing my career, this is one of the best decisions I ever made to aid my mental health.

People-pleasing

Wow, this had to change because I had been at it for years: putting people in front of my needs even if it made me ill. It felt like I had been walking on eggshells all my life. It was exhausting and ate away at my self-worth. I needed therapy for this at the start because I had been doing it for so long it had become a deeply ingrained behaviour. I'll detail just some of the things my people-pleasing led me to do.

- I would have relationships with men because I felt I had to and didn't want to say no.

- I ended up having sex with guys I didn't fancy because they had met me on a date and paid for dinner, so I felt guilty not to. (Gawd, I cringe now at this, and the role alcohol played in providing me with the 'courage' to act in this way.)

- I'd attend work and other social events that I really didn't feel comfortable about going to because I was too scared to say no.

- I put up with verbal abuse and ridicule from others (who claimed it was banter) because I didn't know how to approach it, and maybe I even believed what they were saying.

These are just some of the things that people-pleasing led me to do. It had to change and learning to set boundaries and stick to them helped me shift out of this role.

Seeking Reassurance – I believe this came hand in hand with the people-pleasing and because I was so used to letting others make decisions for me. So I think I fell into the belief that everyone knew better than me. It was especially the case with anxiety as I became dependent on my father to reassure me rather than learn how to reassure myself. I had to work on this, and I started by learning to include myself in my life and ask myself what I wanted, what I needed and not looking to others for the answer.

Rejecting 'blood is thicker than water' – I slowly learnt it's OK to disagree with this phrase. Because for me, it didn't ring true. When I was a people-pleaser, then OK, maybe it did, but once I admitted just how damaging some family relationships were to my emotional wellbeing, then that's when I began to question things.

Our society promotes family as everything, and people who choose not to have certain family members in their lives are deemed emotionally flawed. This is an utter nonsense, if not damaging, mindset to believe. Unfortunately, there will always be people in our lives who aren't good for us; and yes, this can be a parent, sibling, or another relative. That is the sad but hard truth.

Most relationships with my close family were kind-hearted, respectful, and full of genuine love and support. But the ones that were narcissistic, conditional, and manipulative had to change. I knew that to live a life of maximum emotional health and wellbeing, I had to set boundaries and keep them either at a healthy distance or not in my life at all.

It's tough making these kinds of decisions, but after suffering for so long and finally setting out to heal every part of my life, there was no point in me making some positive changes and then leaving this one to continue to impact my mental health for the sake of a phrase.

I can't tell you how much better I began to feel by making all these changes. I gradually felt more empowered and in control of things for the very first time. But, like every behavioural change, it takes time to adjust and settle into the new ways of living your life. These days, however, if I catch myself slipping into old unhelpful habits, I act with compassion and am careful not to beat myself up over it.

Safety Behaviours

We develop safety behaviours because we believe they keep us safe. My two main safety behaviours were: (1) having to carry around specific items, and (2) using avoidance.

The items I could never leave the house without were:

- bottle of water

- 2mg diazepam (just in case)

- chocolate bar

- headache tablets

- tissues

- my mobile phone (I could pretend someone called and needed me to go if I wanted a quick escape)

- earphones

- sunglasses to distance myself from others and even sometimes a safe person.

The key here is learning not to let these items control your recovery. By all means use them at the start of your recovery, when leaving the house seems impossible, but I also discovered it's just as important to gradually leave each item behind (more on this on page 69).

Examples of my avoidance behaviour included:

- driving myself instead of being a passenger

- giving excuses why I couldn't go places, e.g. I had work to finish or had a migraine

- taking the longer route to places that I knew would avoid traffic lights and busy roads.

Did these safety behaviours and items work? If you mean did they provide temporary relief and a false sense of safety? Yes! Or because I believed that they helped me, then they did.

Did they help me recover? No. They just strengthened the belief that I was in danger, took away any chance of believing that I could cope and kept me stuck in the anxiety cycle.

So why did I use them and think I needed them? Because anxiety felt so threatening that I grasped onto anything and everything I thought may help. I didn't want to feel anxious, and so if I believed something could reduce the risk of that, I'd use it. I can now see that I had associated the lack of anxiety I felt or the swiftness of it passing to me using these behaviours. I truly believed they protected and saved me from my worst fear: anxiety. And like with anything, if you believe something enough, it will appear to work for you. And that's the power of beliefs!

The truth is that safety behaviours do not benefit recovery. In fact, they can keep you stuck in the 'I can't cope' mindset. Healing from anxiety is about building up self-belief and taking action to weaken its grip on you and dismantling the limiting beliefs that have kept you stuck in the anxious loop. Unfortunately, holding on to safety behaviours prolonged and hindered my recovery journey because they stole all the credit for keeping me safe.

Self-confidence grows much quicker once you learn to let go of safety behaviours and start taking the credit for your ability to manage, cope, and recover on your own.

Letting go of safety behaviours is something I gradually did while working through my exposure therapy exercises. As my confidence grew, I began to lose these behaviours one by one over time.

You can start by asking yourself what safety behaviours you use and rely on to stay anxiety-free and then ask yourself why you believe they keep you safe. Then, as you progress in your recovery, you can select which behaviour to let go of when you feel ready.

CHAPTER THREE

You Are Not Broken, Damaged, or Crazy

I believe it is so important not to label ourselves as 'anxious people' because it simply isn't true or helpful. For far too long, I thought that I was just an anxious person and would have to live with anxiety and panic disorder forever. But that was a belief that hindered my recovery for quite some time. Comments like 'oh, she's just the anxious type, over-sensitive, and a drama queen' only added to this belief and didn't help.

The more I learnt about anxiety and why we suffer from it, the more I felt that maybe this label I'd placed on myself wasn't true; nor that I had to remain stuck like this forever. What had tried to convince me otherwise was the prognosis from my doctor that came with my diagnosis. It suggested that I was just an anxious person and would be forever!

I was, indeed, suffering from an anxiety and panic disorder, but that was all. Being anxious and highly sensitive wasn't who I was. It was something I was experiencing due to various reasons and circumstances.

Although I had kind of worked it out for myself, in 2015 a conversation with a holistic anxiety therapist confirmed this, which then opened up a whole new world of possibilities for me. The truth was that I had unresolved trauma, was locked in negative and fear-based safety behaviours, was under a lot of stress at home, and in a stressful career that was not fulfilling or kind to my mental health. On top of that, I lived a somewhat unhealthy lifestyle to manage the stress and with low self-worth that I was battling with every day. So it is no wonder I was anxious and appeared highly sensitive.

My suffering had nothing to do with being an anxious person. It was a combination of factors I needed to work through, heal from, and change. And quite frankly, the stigma and need to act as if everything was OK impacted my recovery more than anything. This label of everything being 'fine' meant I felt pressured not to be anxious around others, which only gave me more stress. I am not a fan of faking it until you make it, especially with anxiety. I believe we should be allowed to feel as open and honest with our struggle and receive the support and compassion we deserve, as I am sure this would help so much with people's recovery.

This chapter is to tell you that you are not an anxious person. There will be so many factors contributing to why you are struggling, but I believe that none are unresolvable: even the ones out of your control you can choose to leave behind. Just, please, lose any label that suggests your struggle with anxiety is who you are as a person and give yourself the time and space to heal. Also, ignore the stigma that comes with mental ill health and start making the radical changes I discussed earlier to what you know has kept you stuck or held your recovery back.

Your life matters. You matter, so make that your priority. Recovery from anxiety is obtainable. You just need to believe it. You must understand that even though you may feel broken, damaged, or unfixable when suffering from anxiety, you are not. Knowing and accepting this is essential for recovery. You are experiencing an over-sensitised nervous system, mental fatigue, and emotional exhaustion, all of which can be healed, and recovery achieved. These are not permanent states, and although they cause distress, they cannot hurt you.

I spent years thinking I was broken and damaged because nobody told me any different. I also began to feel more and more unfixable after every 'anxiety cure' that failed to end my struggle. I tried almost everything on the market to fix myself, remove anxiety from my life, and get my old self back, but nothing worked. I visited 'anxiety experts' who claimed they could cure me in just a couple of sessions, went on retreats that claimed they would banish anxiety and change my life. Then there were the online programmes, expensive email support from 'experts'... you name it, I tried it. Sometimes I got some temporary relief, but anxiety would always return, and I would be left feeling unfixable and deflated.

There were a few things I didn't know back then, like (1) I didn't need fixing, (2) only I could heal myself with the correct guidance and support, and (3) I needed the time and space that would allow me to heal properly. It was these three points that changed the direction of my recovery journey. I learnt that the things I had tried to 'fix' my anxiety with hadn't worked because they couldn't possibly ever work. Healing anxiety is an inside job that requires the sufferer to take action while showing courage, commitment, and effort. Taking action means resting, changing, learning facts, unlearning unhealthy behaviours and thinking patterns, and exposure. The truth is, no one can heal you, but they can guide, support, and encourage you to recovery.

Another thing I didn't realise was that healing anxiety takes time; it takes time to understand and accept what's happening to you, learn the facts, and shift your perception from one of fear to one of knowing you can recover. Anxiety can't hurt you, make you go crazy, or worse, but it can negatively impact your life if you fear it. You need space to heal because when you try to recover while simultaneously juggling numerous other aspects in life, it is much more difficult. Having space to heal is also necessary as it allows an already overstretched mind the chance to rest and settle.

Support and encouragement is essential. Having a person or persons in your corner showing you compassion, love, and encouragement can be so empowering. At times, it's a tough road, so this kind of support will help so often that. So, please, lose the words 'broken' and 'unfixable' from your vocabulary when it comes to your struggle with anxiety. Swap them for 'mentally and emotionally exhausted' and 'I'm in the process of healing', because these are much more accurate with what's going on.

Am I Going Crazy?

'Going crazy' was my number one fear. I spent years worrying that I was losing my mind. Even after I'd learnt everything I possibly could about anxiety, it took me a long while to stop questioning my sanity because the symptoms would be so intense that my only conclusion was that I was losing my mind. Here's what I learnt.

This fear initially came from not knowing what was happening to me and not understanding how anxiety can cause incredibly intense and scary symptoms. The fear of losing your mind is one of the most common fears. It comes from the extremely high emotions, the adrenaline rush, and the overwhelming feeling of losing control when experiencing intense anxiety. Again, if we had learnt about this at an early age, we might have been better prepared for it. But as many of us didn't, when it does happen, the intensity of how it feels is so alien to us that we automatically think the worst, e.g. that we are going insane or dying.

What helped me dismantle this fear was to learn about anxiety symptoms, why they happen, how they affect the body and mind, and most importantly, why they are not a sign of insanity. So, for example, I first learnt how adrenaline and cortisol (the stress hormones) can produce a range of intense symptoms when high levels are present in the body for prolonged periods. This includes symptoms of racing thoughts, derealisation, blurred vision, inability to concentrate, and brain fog – all signs that made me feel as if I was losing my mind. What started to reassure me was that I could find no evidence anywhere that anxiety can cause you to lose your mind. Indeed, while I repeatedly found that these chemicals can cause distress and intense discomfort, I discovered they are not actually harmful.

There was another moment that I will never forget, which planted a more personal seed of reassurance within me. It was when my father – an incredibly wise guy who had worked in an environment for decades where he witnessed people struggling with high emotions daily – told me, 'Lisa, if you were losing your mind, you wouldn't be concerned about it as you wouldn't know.' I can't tell you how much comfort this gave me.

Although learning about how and why anxiety exists won't cure you, it can help you overcome your fear and stop you from being tricked into what the anxious mind suggests is happening to you. For example, before learning about anxiety as thoroughly as I did, I constantly worried about losing my mind, yet it never occurred in the 20 years of suffering from anxiety. Instead, I got distressed, highly overwhelmed, and upset, but I didn't lose my mind or even come close to it.

I hope sharing this brings you comfort and helps stop you from adding to your worries about what you are experiencing. Symptoms of stress and anxiety are just that: symptoms. They are not a sign of anything other than experiencing high anxiety levels and will dissipate once the cause of the anxiety has been either healed or overcome. So, instead of adding fear to how you feel, use that energy to discover the cause of the anxiety and not waste it worrying about the symptoms.

CHAPTER FOUR

What Anxiety Is and What It Isn't

What Is Anxiety and Why Can It Become A Problem?

I want to remind you that I am not a medical professional or a therapist. But I have learnt a lot about anxiety and developed a deep understanding after struggling with it for decades. So I feel confident that sharing what I have learnt over the years can help others recover from their fear of anxiety disorder. I have written this from my own experience.

It would help if you first accept that anxiety is a natural human emotion designed to keep you safe. It is a response that occurs when wellbeing is under threat. But so many of us don't realise this when we first experience anxiety, so we interpret it as something terrible. And so, we begin to fear it, which then develops into a disorder.

Although it may feel life or sanity-threatening, it is not. Nor is it a disease, a monster, or a defect in the brain. Anxiety is not an illness you catch or something that attacks you out of nowhere. It's an entirely natural physiological response. The sickness is our fear of it and this is when the problems and the suffering begins.

Once the fear of anxiety exists, it creates a secondary fear that fuels and exaggerates it. The brain sees this secondary fear as a threat and responds the only way it knows how: by releasing more anxiety because it needs us to take note and flee the threat. The initial burst of anxiety would have undoubtedly subsided without this secondary fear. But because of the secondary fear to the brain, the threat never goes away, so an anxious cycle develops, and it is this cycle that negatively impacts your life and can lead to anxiety disorder.

Things that can trigger anxiety (apart from a genuine threat like a raging bear chasing you) are prolonged stress, mental exhaustion, sudden or unresolved trauma, substance abuse, illness, and a fear of anxiety. The brain can interpret these as threats depending on their severity and longevity.

An example of anxiety in action when there's a genuine threat to your wellbeing:

You are crossing a road when suddenly a car appears out of nowhere, speeding towards you. You immediately run to safety. The reaction that propelled you to safety resulted from anxiety: the fight-or-flight response. In those split seconds, your heart rate went up, your thoughts raced, muscles tensed, and your awareness heightened. Anxiety did its job, and once you were on the other side of the road, safe and sound, the response dissipated. You may have felt shaken afterwards, but that's normal considering you had a close call with a speeding car and a body full of adrenaline.

Now an example of a perceived threat:

You are thinking about going for a walk, but you're scared of feeling anxious and not coping. A friend persuades you that you'll be fine, so you set off. Your mind senses your apprehension and starts spurting out lots of 'what if' thoughts and scenarios that you focus on. Your brain interprets this as a threat as if what you fear is happening. And so, the brain releases anxiety to keep you safe. You feel the effects of the anxiety release and start to worry more, confirming your fears and strengthening your belief that you can't do things because anxiety will show up and you can't cope. You run home, and only there do you find relief.

In the last example, there was no real threat, just a fear of one, and that fear triggered the anxiety. So the only difference between the actual threat example and the perceived one is that the perceived threat never has the chance to pass because it is in your thoughts, and your attention to it keeps it alive.

Now, I know we don't like hearing that we are bringing the suffering on ourselves. Our fear of anxiety is what the brain perceives as a threat and the more we respond in fear to anxiety the stronger this becomes and the more mentally and emotionally deflated we become. Essentially, the threat is internal and so never has chance to pass unless we take action to face it.

Feeling anxious is only ever meant to be a short-lived response. But continuous fear results in a constant threat, so the fight-or-flight response goes into overdrive. As a result, the body reacts with a continual anxiety flow, producing intense and sometimes severe symptoms.

I genuinely believe – and have said it many times over the years – that if we had been taught about mental and emotional health at an early age, a lot of the unnecessary mental suffering that many find themselves in could have been avoided. I'm so pleased that mental health is finally on the school curriculum. Even so, I still feel our approach and acceptance of mental health disorders is changing too slowly.

Why You Don't Have to Fear Anxiety

If you're struggling with anxiety because you fear it, losing that fear and the dread surrounding it is key to recovery. Few things make you want to escape and avoid more than anxiety and the sense of apprehension and worry that something terrible is about to happen. Anxiety sometimes shows up for a specific reason, such as a first date, job interview, or dental appointment. But it can also appear out of nowhere and for no reason. One thing we can all agree on is that we don't like the feeling and want it to go away. So we'll do almost anything to get rid of it, and this is where avoidance behaviour starts.

The desire to escape or avoid anxiety is very natural. After all, anxiety is a warning signal to let us know there's a threat and we need to protect ourselves. It is also a bodily response that does a fantastic job at helping us stay alive. Imagine if a bear was chasing you in the woods, then the fight-or-flight response of a racing heart and shortness of breath is what prepares you to flee, fight, or freeze: it is what you need to escape the bear!

Anxiety becomes a problem when we become fearful of it. This fear can trigger the response routinely, causing 'false alarms' around situations, thoughts, and people that are not a genuine threat. It's why so many of us turn to avoidance behaviour because we believe it protects us. But it doesn't, it just adds another fear to your list and reinforces your belief that anxiety is dangerous. And so, we become intolerant of uncertainty, and our world becomes smaller. The fact is, we don't know what the future holds, but it is rarely a better choice to avoid stuff for fear something terrible will happen than to go ahead and see how it pans out!

Anxiety is, without a doubt, uncomfortable, distressing, and scary, but it cannot hurt you. Even high levels of anxiety – such as panic attacks – can't hurt you. They couldn't possibly because they are a type of threat response designed to keep you out of harm's way. That is all they are. But what can hurt you is your fear of anxiety because it stops you from enjoying life. Because, let's be honest, living life in continuous fear and repeatedly avoiding situations is no fun at all – I know this because I lived that life for decades.

As I probably repeat many times in this book, to break free of this anxious cycle is to start seeing anxiety for what it is and not what your anxious mind tells you it is. It's the starting point for recovery and getting your life back to how you want it to be. Only then, as you begin to try new things, will your world become bigger again and you'll start surprising yourself with what you can do, while learning that anxiety is not something you need to fear.

Unfortunately, when we experience anxiety without this knowledge (like I did), we stop living and let our fear of anxiety take over and make all our decisions. Approximately 1 in 4 people will have a mental health problem in their lifetime, with 6 in 100 experiencing generalised anxiety disorder (GAD). I am sure that statistic is higher, but the stigma attached to mental health, unfortunately, still prevents people from coming forward and getting the help and support they need. It's so sad because although anxiety is distressing and uncomfortable, it can be treated and a fear of it overcome. You can get to a place where you don't feel you need to escape or avoid situations that make you anxious, because you have learnt to tolerate the discomfort and removed your fear of it.

It's where I am today. I still get anxious, of course I do. But I don't get anxious unnecessarily or experience those false warnings that used to dictate my life. I no longer have a fear of fear and so if anxiety does show up it does so and passes quickly because there is no longer that secondary fear that for years kept it hanging around and lingering longer than necessary.

CHAPTER FIVE

Anxiety Symptoms

This chapter is all about symptoms. Over the years I wasted far too much time on trying to fix the symptoms when what I should have done was work on losing my fear of anxiety and then the symptoms would have disappeared on their own.

But we often become entangled in and very concerned about the symptoms we experience while suffering from anxiety. Unfortunately, it's these symptoms that we dwell on and misinterpret, that push us into a negative mindset of believing we are going crazy, are seriously ill, or worse. All the symptoms mentioned below are ones I personally experienced. They would trick me over and over again into thinking that there was something seriously wrong with me. This list isn't exhaustive, but these symptoms were the ones that caused me the most distress:

- panic attacks (sudden bursts of fear and intense unease that seemed to come out of nowhere)

- derealisation (feeling detached from the world and everything around me, like I was in a weird and scary dream state)

- muffled hearing (as if I was wearing earmuffs)

- tense neck and shoulders

- tight throat (sometimes a burning sensation and unable to speak)

- lack of concentration

- a deep sense of unease

- anxious or intrusive thoughts

- dizziness

- loss of appetite

- inability to relax

- night terrors (disturbed sleep, waking up full of panic)

- mental and physical fatigue

- diarrhoea

- dry mouth

- blurred vision

- heart palpitations

- hot, sweating head

- trembles

- paranoia

- inability to feel safe (even when I was hugged or reassured, I felt nothing but fear).

The countless times I was convinced I needed medical attention or a trip to A&E, the symptoms were so convincing that even after the all-clear from a doctor, I'd still sit worrying and overthinking them and doubting what my doctor said. Which was always, 'It's anxiety, Lisa, these are a result of the anxiety you are experiencing!'

It's difficult to accept this diagnosis because the symptoms are incredibly debilitating at times; intense and distressing. But remember that adrenaline can have a massive effect on the body and cause all sorts of strange and uncomfortable symptoms. And it is not just adrenaline that impacts how we feel. Our cortisol levels, too, can cause intense feelings of unease, but (as with all chemicals released when our nervous system is over-stimulated) they are only there to protect us.

The thing to remember about symptoms is that although they feel terrifying and distressing, they cannot hurt you! Just look at how many times you've experienced them, and you're still here. This is proof that they are not harmful, and you can handle them. Just don't waste your time focusing on the symptoms and fixing them. Instead, put your energy into overcoming your fear of anxiety, the false beliefs that are tricking you, as it is usually these that are causing the anxiety in the first place. Overcoming these will help reduce anxiety levels, and the symptoms will gradually disappear.

Suppose you have had the all-clear from the doctor regarding the symptoms concerning you. In that case, dwelling on them further will only worsen the anxiety. It is better to accept that your body will produce uncomfortable symptoms when anxiety levels are high. The best way to resolve the symptoms is to lower your anxiety levels because you will only get the relief you crave once you do.

My biggest fear was losing my sanity. The drastic change in my personality convinced me of that. So how did I go from an outgoing, confident woman to this shell of a person riddled with fear? My conclusion was that I had to be going insane. But 25 years later, I still had my sanity after years of panic attacks and periods of chronic GAD. Even though I had felt at times like I was going crazy, it never actually happened. The truth is I was experiencing heightened levels of adrenaline and an overwhelmed and highly sensitised nervous system that produced symptoms that made me feel like I was going crazy.

I am sure if you are reading this, you will resonate, and if you're being totally honest with yourself, you will also see that your worst fear about how you are feeling hasn't materialised either. A tip for you to use while experiencing anxiety and becoming overly concerned about symptoms is to always look outside your anxious thoughts for the evidence.

Think about what your non-anxious self or a trusted loved one would say and feel.

Why Is Anxiety Worse in The Mornings?

Anxiety can be so common in the morning because the stress hormone, cortisol, is highest in the first hour upon waking, helping us to stay alert and focused. However, going to bed feeling anxious can also cause cortisol levels to spike too early, which might lead you to wake up anxious. In addition, blood sugar levels (which are lower first thing in the morning) and possible dehydration can both create a sense of unease upon wakening.

Morning anxiety was once the bane of my life. There was a time I'd wake almost every morning full of panic, dread, and a sense of doom. Falling asleep was never a real issue. Instead, it was always a few seconds after waking that would cause me the most distress.

It was Dr Weekes's book, *Self Help for Your Nerves*, that taught me all I needed to know about morning anxiety. It validated how I was feeling and advised me how to manage morning anxiety. It was such a comfort to find something that explained why my mornings were usually full of panic.

Her main advice was to 'rise when you wake'.

Don't lie in bed dwelling on how you feel and start analysing it. Instead, get up, open the curtains, jump in the shower, put the radio on, and have a cup of tea. 'The main thing is to make some quick effort as soon as you open your eyes, so that early morning depression [or anxiety] cannot establish itself.'

Taking the advice of getting – and sticking to – a morning routine stopped me from slipping down the rabbit hole of distress. It takes practice, but the brain eventually learns that mornings are no longer a time for fear, when you stick with it. I also drink a glass of cold water upon wakening as I find it wakes my whole body up and gives me a refreshing feeling, which is much better than that sluggish feeling, which, again, can suck you into negative thinking.

Even if you don't feel like it at first, start looking at mornings as a new day, a fresh start, and a building block for the day ahead. If you continue to fear the mornings and associate them with anxiety, you'll continue to struggle. Accept this new approach, knowing at first the pull to fall into the anxious sensations, checking in on yourself, and giving into anxious thoughts will be strong, but stick to it by getting up and carrying on with your morning routine. I promise you that your determination and commitment to stick to it will bring an end to your morning anxiety.

My Experience with The Symptom 'Derealisation'

I started to experience derealisation (DR) when my anxiety was at an all-time high. I can only describe it as feeling like I was no longer a part of this world. Like I was in a scary dream-like state where nothing looked or felt real. It was incredibly scary and distressing.

While experiencing DR nothing appeared real; people appeared in slow motion, as if they were blurry. I felt deaf, and the environment would swirl slowly around me. It felt like I was completely detached from my surroundings which compounded my fear of going crazy. Luckily, these periods of DR didn't last very long, but they did keep reoccurring throughout my struggle with anxiety.

I later learnt that DR comes from an overloaded, stressed out, and overwhelmed mind and, to protect itself, the brain draws on its inbuilt safety mechanism to slow things down. It is taking its wellbeing into its own hands. I genuinely believe it does this when it sees little to no chance of any respite coming from our worrying or any indication we are trying to fix behaviours. It's not dangerous or a cause for concern. It's just your brain telling you that enough is enough and that it needs a break.

Our minds are savvier than we think when suffering from anxiety. It has tried to get us to slow down, rest, and maybe change our lifestyle, yet we continue to ignore the signs, e.g. anxiety, stress, mental fatigue.

Your behaviours and perception of anxiety have created a new problem – your fear of anxiety. You've given the brain even more things to do, like considering why you feel this way and how to fix it. But unfortunately, it's also put your mind and nervous system under more stress, even higher than it was when you first started struggling with anxiety. This additional pressure has made you feel worse, spiralling into an anxiety disorder where anxiety becomes the only thing you can focus on. Your days are spent worrying about anxiety: how to avoid it, and how to rid yourself of it.

When this happens, the mind becomes so overwhelmed that it decides to shut things down and take control in a last attempt to grab some rest. So how did I eventually deal with it? I dealt with it the same way I learnt to deal with all my anxiety symptoms: by not making them important. I learnt that when the brain sees that these feelings caused me fear, it interpreted that fear as a threat. But when I went about my day regardless of the symptoms I was experiencing, the brain saw that the threat had passed and so settled down. This takes practice!

Regardless of the symptoms, in order to overcome an anxiety disorder, we must show the brain that we are not in danger. We can only do this by carrying on with whatever we are doing, regardless of how we feel. Without giving the symptoms our attention and making them important, the brain will stop seeing and reacting to them as a threat. If you are struggling with derealisation or depersonalisation, please be reassured that it is not harmful or a sign that you are going crazy. The trick is to not overthink it as this then gives the symptom a meaning and that meaning gets interpreted as a threat.

Here is a tip that helped me no end in my recovery and with those periods of derealisation. Don't get disappointed when you have days where your symptoms are intense. Just accept that you feel crap and stay busy: carrying on as normal will tell your brain you are safe. But, also, when you have a good day, don't make it a huge, big deal either! This will then teach the brain that anxiety is not important, in either positive or negative terms. It also helps put anxious thoughts and feelings into perspective and allows them to fade away and disappear, which is what all thoughts do when we don't focus on them. I found that recovery is about teaching your brain that feelings of anxiety, no matter how intense, are ultimately not that important.

My Experience with Generalised Anxiety Disorder

Although I suffered from panic attacks, it was GAD that caused me the most anguish over the years. The panic attacks, although scary, would come and go far quicker, whereas GAD would hang around and plague me all day, every day for weeks and months at a time. Once I experienced it for ten months flat. I forgot what it felt like to feel unafraid and calm. It was also in these long periods of GAD that I'd experience derealisation. It was extremely challenging, and I have tremendous empathy for anyone going through the same!

My panic attacks would come and go pretty quickly and leave me worn out for the rest of the day. But GAD was a completely different ball game because it would linger like a thick cloud of fear, making me feel trapped. It would even bleed into my comfort zone and disrupt every sense of security I thought I had.

When GAD stayed for prolonged periods, I would opt for medication to give me some breathing space. There is nothing wrong with taking medication. I have done so, and I believe it has saved my life to this day. However, I would say to always try to combine it with therapy so that the breathing space benefits your recovery!

I believe GAD developed in me because of my unresolved trauma and ignoring the stress and emotional overload signals while navigating through my life. It kept pushing me into these periods of excessive worrying and feelings of guilt. I knew I needed the support of a professional for this because trying to outrun it was no longer working. But I kept putting it off as long as I could, numbing it with alcohol and praying it would go away. But it didn't, so I caved in, and again, went to see a specialist.

My fear of panic attacks and anticipatory anxiety I felt I could overcome by myself with gradual exposure practice under the guidance of Dr Weekes's books and practising CBT (cognitive behavioural therapy) that I learnt from a previous therapist. But GAD needed me to stop, take a step back, learn how to soothe myself, and do some profound inner unravelling of my belief system and former self-limiting stories. I needed to work with a therapist on this to enable me to heal fully.

If you're struggling with GAD, the first thing to do is to give yourself some time out from 'doing': see your doctor, and reach out for some help and support. Doing these things helped me settle and move forward from GAD. If you are unable to or simply don't want to see a therapist then you check out an experienced therapist who specialises in anxiety online. Some of my favourites on Instagram are Dr Susanne Wolf @Mymentalhealthspace for mental health in general, Dr Jenn @the.anxiety.doc. as an anxiety specialist., Nicole Perla @the.holistic.psychologist for everything holistic and Dr Kirren @DRKIRREN for health anxiety These are my go-to if I need specialist information and facts.

CHAPTER SIX

Anxiety Recovery and What I Learnt

How Long Does It Take to Recover?

I get asked this so often, and my answer is always the same – you can't put a time frame on it. Recovery takes as long as it takes, and this is because it is dependent on a few things. First, it depends on what is the cause of your anxiety. It may require therapy to dismantle and resolve it if it is unresolved trauma. Then there is the role you play, which may need you to slow down, make some lifestyle changes, and allow yourself to heal. Another area you may need to focus on, especially if your anxiety has been chronic, is learning how to soothe yourself. The nervous system and your anxious mind can only settle without further stimulation through additional fear. I know in my case, I was nowhere near ready to try exposure therapy until I had taken time out, learnt to soothe myself, and educated myself on the facts about anxiety to alter my perspective and mindset about it. If I hadn't done these things, I would undoubtedly still be suffering to this day because my fear of anxiety would have remained.

One of the key things I struggled with while healing was impatience. I just wanted to feel normal NOW, and at first, I dismissed any advice that told me to slow down, accept the feelings, and trust the process. I didn't want to do that. I wanted a quick fix, magic pill, or miracle cure (which don't exist, by the way), so if you feel like this: trust me, I get it!

But I learnt relatively quickly that anxiety and impatience are closely linked because feeling anxious makes it hard to wait for relief to happen. As a result, you start questioning the symptoms, envying other people who appear to have their life sorted, and beat yourself up, which sinks you deeper into those anxious thoughts. So, you see, all impatience does is create more anxiety. Also, when you focus ONLY on the negatives of a situation, you will think stuff like 'Why can't I just do XYZ?' instead of saying to yourself, 'I'm healing and working towards doing XYZ, and if it takes a bit of time, that's OK!' You'll only feel worse if you tell yourself how you should be feeling.

When you begin to accept that anxiety recovery takes time, you will have a much smoother ride while doing it. Never feel pressured into forcing yourself, even if you're having therapy or following the words of someone like Dr Weekes. By all means, listen closely to what they suggest and do the work.

But always go at your own pace, remove all expectations, and shower yourself with kindness and compassion, being proud of every step you take, no matter how small. Please don't allow your urgency to ruin your healing journey or progress. Remember, impatience takes up so much mental energy but doesn't change or improve anything. All it does is add to your suffering and hinder recovery.

Anxiety Recovery Is More Than Just Doing Exposure Therapy

I soon realised that recovering from anxiety wasn't just about facing your fears. It's also about taking a close look at other things like your relationships, environment, behaviours, and expectations.

Even when you do exposure therapy or CBT or whatever you use to overcome your anxiety disorder, if you remain in circumstances that fuel insecurity, negativity, stress, unease, and low self-worth, then it's going to be a real challenge for you.

It wasn't until I started this journey that I began to see how things that I used to think were 'just the way it is', were actually matters I could and should remove from my life. When I finally became radically honest with myself, I accepted that blood isn't thicker than water. Relationships should nourish and not complicate things. Other people's expectations are not something to make yourself ill over, resulting from your own needs being ignored.

Society's conditioning has a nasty way of impairing our inner peace by perpetuating the message 'it is what it is,' which is bullshit. I found that society can make you sick and keep you sick if you don't recognise this. If something weighs heavily on you and doesn't support your emotional wellbeing or recovery, permit yourself to let it go.

I tried multiple times to overcome my anxiety disorder and failed because I still thought I had to please others. I was still in the mindset of 'it is what it is' when things were stressful and unkind, thinking I was the one who was weak and damaged. But that is not true. We don't have to put up with things and neglect our needs. If recovery isn't working and we find ourselves battling anxiety, we have to stop and seriously look at what isn't working for us in life and make some changes. And that is what I did to finally recover.

If you are willing to do the work, make some changes, and put your mental and emotional health first, you can 100% recover. Then, with the right choices, you can maintain a relatively anxiety-free life. I say relatively because, as humans, there will be times you experience anxiety, which is OK. The difference is that because you no longer fear anxiety, you don't prolong any odd periods of feeling anxious and therefore don't hinder your recovery.

When I finally felt ready to take my recovery seriously, it became exciting as I took a holistic approach, so my whole world changed for the better. Since there were no real-life holistic therapists available at the same time as I felt ready to see one, I decided to combine reliable sources of information and practices to ensure I was incorporating the body, mind, and soul in my healing. In addition to Dr Weekes's books and my CBT, this included following people like Dr Nicole LePera @the.holistic.psychologist, reading *An Untethered Soul* by Michael Alan Singer, and attending Buddhist mindfulness sessions.

My anxiety began to melt away, and my self-worth grew. Before this, I'd just patched myself up and hung onto those relatively anxiety-free moments until the inevitable happened. The patches fell off, which happened again and again.

My recovery originally existed around temporary relief and falling back into all the bad habits, mental fatigue, and stress that had caused my anxiety in the first place. It was the same cycle for many, many years. Temporary relief, stress, bad lifestyle choices, trying to plod on, illness, and burnout, back to sickness, then trying to patch myself up again and back to temporary relief. It was never a proper recovery.

This time was different. I wanted to break the anxiety and unhealthy cycle that kept me defaulting to a sick and anxious person. To do that, I had to make changes in my life, set boundaries, do some inner work on my life script (belief system), and overcome my fear of anxiety. This combination is what saved me from spending a further 15-20 years battling anxiety and led me to my recovery and freedom today.

I have lived my life these past few years without the concern or fear of anxiety. That's pretty awesome for someone who spent close to 20 years living in fear and worry. I can now do things and feel good, and that's all that matters. I am also extremely protective over my mental health and made a commitment to myself to never allow anything or anyone to impact it negatively again. I put self-care first. If I am faced with something emotionally challenging, I speak out and get support. If someone brings drama my way or I feel their presence is making me feel uncomfortable because I cannot be my true self, I now walk away. Feeling good again and happy means everything to me because I never thought I would be able to experience or say that. But down to my hard work and commitment to my recovery, I can, and it feels so good after living life trapped in an anxious mind for decades. My aim now is to help others do and feel the same.

Different Approaches for Recovery

I often talk about how exposure therapy helped me recover, and that's true. But reassurance, soothing, medication, time out, and self-help did too.

You see, I found there will be times when you need soothing and other times all you need is a gentle push. For example, when I was experiencing periods of chronic anxiety, there was absolutely no way on earth I could have attempted exposure therapy because I could barely function doing my everyday things. What I needed in those times was reassurance, comfort, and some self-soothing to help reduce my anxiety levels. It was in these periods of chronic anxiety that I would use medication to help. And once I felt stronger and more able to do the hard work to combat my fears, then I would.

In my periods of GAD and high-functioning anxiety, I would feel anxious but try to carry on regardless by using unhealthy coping methods like alcohol and overworking. Not a smart move, but at the time, I was hoping anxiety would disappear on its own. But unfortunately, that doesn't happen. So, I needed to take time out and own my recovery by making some lifestyle changes, putting my energy into soothing myself, slowing down, and working on facing my fears.

I also went through periods of what I called 'dormant anxiety' where I didn't experience anxiety that much, but my fear of it remained. These periods were short-lived. They occurred when I was deeply involved in something, e.g. a work project or something that took up all my attention. But there was always a part of me fearing anxiety's return, so avoidance was still my number one coping behaviour, which, of course, kept anxiety simmering away in the background.

Seeing as anxiety can have different intensity levels, combining different healing approaches seems more sensible. In my experience, this was a much more effective way to heal than the 'one-way suits all' approach that some swear by. There were so many times I had sessions with therapists who would push 'one-way suits all' which left me feeling lost and doubtful of their methods. They made me feel that my need for soothing and reassurance was wrong, which added to my low self-worth. Then there were the therapists who only wanted to soothe and talk. They'd avoid any conversation about exposure or actively facing my fears. Instead, it was all about going over my past, and written homework. It was not their fault and probably may suit some people, but it didn't work for me.

It was after following all these unsuccessful or stagnant therapy sessions that I started looking into a holistic approach that I could combine with the works of Dr Weekes, and it was here that everything started to make sense and fall into place.

I learnt how to self-soothe, nurture, and care for my emotional and mental wellbeing before progressing to how to challenge and gradually push myself to work through my fears. It was the combination of therapy I needed, and my recovery blossomed.

So, this detailed chapter is really about knowing that if you've been having therapy and it isn't working or resonating with you, it is OK to change that. It's OK to leave a therapist for one you are more suited to. It is OK to ask for reassurance and self-soothing advice. It is OK to tailor your recovery to a way that ticks all the boxes that you need ticking.

It is also about knowing that there is not just one way anxiety can affect us.

We are all different and will have different reasons for why anxiety became a problem in the first place for us.

The core wound (as I called it) that fuelled my anxiety (I am not talking about the secondary fear of fear) was my belief that I was not good enough. Every negative and stressful experience just latched onto this and fed it. If I had ignored this core wound and only done my exposure therapy and focused solely on my fear of anxiety, my recovery wouldn't have come as quickly as it did. Within the holistic approach I took, I managed to learn the facts about anxiety so I could change my perception of it and overcome my fear of it. Secondary to this, the holistic approach allowed me to tackle the profound work on the 'lack of self-worth' core wound that could no longer be ignored. To this day, I am still nurturing and healing that core wound, but because the secondary fear that caused anxiety to trigger unnecessarily within me no longer exists, I have the energy and resources to address this trauma.

For understanding anxiety, exposure therapy, and secondary fear, my go-to is and always will be Dr Weekes. For self-soothing my favourite therapist is Emma Garrick @the.anxiety.whisperer and for holistic and deep healing, @the.anxiety.whisperer Dr Nicole LePera @the.holistic.psychologist .

My Thoughts on Exposure Therapy

I think we all learn pretty quickly that the one thing that keeps us trapped in an anxious cycle is our resistance and battle with anxiety. These behaviours are the default reaction when we experience high anxiety levels with little to no knowledge of what is happening. Anxiety feels so terrifying and extremely uncomfortable that we automatically try to flee from it. It's not something most of us learnt about or spoke about growing up, so it hits us like a ton of bricks. We usually only get to know about anxiety after it has started wreaking havoc in our lives and our nervous system is completely overwhelmed.

By the time I'd started learning about anxiety, I'd already developed behaviours and beliefs that created more anxiety and kept me stuck in the anxious cycle – and I imagine many of you will have or have had the same experience. It's how my battle with anxiety started in the 1990s. Before this, I had no idea that anxiety was a 'thing' or could cause so much damage to my everyday life. So, naturally, it was a complete shock and so scary that my default reaction when I encountered it was to fight it.

I lived like this on and off for decades, white-knuckling and fighting my way through life. I thought of nothing else. I never thought about doing anything other than fighting and struggling with it. What else could I do? No one told me that all the struggling and resisting was keeping me stuck, and so that's what I did.

My breakthrough came when I stumbled across Dr Weekes's book, *Self Help for Your Nerves*. While searching for another cure online (I say another as I'd tried so many already), I came across an article about Dr Weekes. It was about how her teachings had and continued to help people reach a full recovery from anxiety disorders. I couldn't believe it as it was the first time I'd even heard of the possibility of fully recovering from this hell, rather than just learning how to cure the symptoms. I knew I'd been grasping at straws trying to find a cure as I had been scammed so many times in the past on guaranteed treatments that didn't work.

And now, what seemed like out of nowhere came this woman. She was an Australian scientist and doctor who'd helped thousands of people to recover from anxiety. Why hadn't I heard of her? I don't know. But after reading her book, I just knew that this was the breakthrough I so desperately needed, and although her book was published in the 1960s, it felt fresh and full of hope, along with a validation of what I was experiencing, and common sense.

Dr Weekes's book was the first time I was taught to go towards anxious feelings rather than run away from them. To overcome your fear of anxiety, she said you must 'face, accept, float, and let time pass,' which means not running from but staying with the anxious feelings, resistance-free until it has run its course. Her book also explained why it is OK to experience anxious feelings, why they are not harmful, and why exposing yourself to the anxiety without resistance or fear will lead to recovery. This approach was all new to me but brought great hope.

My only concern about this approach was that by then I had 15 years of doing the complete opposite under my belt – 15 years of avoidance, suppressing, self-medicating, and white-knuckling to keep safe from anxiety. So, at first, the very thought of staying with the anxious feelings scared the shit out of me. But I thought, 'What have I got to lose?' along with the possibility of, 'I have everything to gain'. I knew that I certainly didn't want to spend a further 15 years struggling my way through life. So I had to give it a go.

What I Found by Doing Exposure Therapy

The thing about exposure therapy, whether you follow someone like Dr Weekes, or have the guidance of another therapist, is that it only works if done correctly. And that is where many of us, including myself, go wrong when we first attempt it. We almost always enter it hoping that anxiety doesn't show up and with an intense fear of what will happen if it does. We fail to realise that the sole purpose of exposure is to feel the anxiety to become desensitised to it and change our reaction to it. Allowing yourself to feel the way you do is not about trying to feel better. Instead, it is about allowing whatever shows up to show up and pass all by itself. It is about letting go of the struggle, resistance, avoidance, and overthinking – all the unhelpful behaviours that encourage anxiety to intensify and hang around. It's about you seeing truth in why anxiety cannot hurt you, always passes, and that you can cope through it.

To be free of anxious feelings, you must be willing to feel them; this is how we become free of the hold they have on us. Educating yourself on this (I recommend you start with Dr Weekes for this) will give you the knowledge to empower yourself and keep you focused. And remember that it is better to spend a few months allowing yourself to experience the discomfort of the anxious feelings so you can heal than to spend a lifetime trying to manage, suppress, and avoid them. I kept that reminder at the front of my mind while doing exposure therapy. And over time, I began to trust the process, and my willingness to do and feel anything that would help me break free from my anxious prison grew stronger.

The only way to break your fear of anxiety is to go towards the anxious feelings willingly, stop avoiding places and situations because of how you feel, and stop trying to feel anything other than what you actually feel at any given time. If you feel anxious, allow yourself to feel anxious. These feelings will never overtake you if you surrender to them and realise that they will always pass.

What Helped Me Do Exposure Therapy Correctly?

Firstly, by educating myself on the facts about anxiety (not what my anxious mind was telling me) and how this approach (where you gradually expose yourself to the fear) works. I chose to use Dr Weekes as my teacher because I could understand and resonate with how she explained things. I genuinely believe it is a great advantage to find someone (it doesn't have to be in person) you connect and resonate with to guide you through anxiety recovery. Out of all the therapists I had seen over the years, I'd never had such confidence or trust in them as I did with Dr Weekes, and I only knew her through her book. I admit it took me some time to get my head around the fact that I needed to feel the anxiety and stay with it. I couldn't try hoping anxiety didn't show up. I had to try hoping it would.

The next challenge was stopping myself from fleeing at the first sign of anxiety or talking myself out of going somewhere that would likely cause anxious thoughts in the first place. But I knew I was in safe hands, and as I said earlier, I had nothing to lose.

To help me, I had made a safety toolkit, the items I always took with me that I mentioned on pages 29-30. Remember, it doesn't hinder having safety tools at the start of exposure therapy because, if you are like me and have suffered for many years, it can help. So, for me, it felt like the sensible thing to do as I wasn't ready for complete flooding or going at it cold turkey. And as you progress, you can then start reducing the safety tools one by one.

My safety tools were:

- bottle of water

- snacks (bag of almonds, chocolate bar, apple, packet of mints)

- paracetamol and ibuprofen

- peppermint aromatherapy oil (I found this soothed me)

- Dr Weekes's book on Audible (for reassurance and guidance), plus the paperback version

- 2mg of Diazepam

- packet of tissues (I was so fearful of needing the toilet)

- pack of handmade 'inspirational quotes'

- notebook and pen (so I could write while practising).

Some may disagree and tell you to ditch all your safety tools before attempting exposure therapy. But I say, this is your recovery and how you approach it is your choice. Yes, you will need to learn how to get comfortable with the discomfort without safety tools eventually, but if taking things for reassurance and comfort will help you initially, then I think it's OK. Just keep an eye out for not being able to relinquish any or all items from your safety toolkit.

Exposure therapy is not about flooding yourself. It is completely different to flooding. Flooding is a completely different method and one I would have only attempted in the presence of a trained and experienced anxiety therapist. Exposure, on the other hand, is something that should be done gradually and at your own pace. And it must be done consistently, with the willingness to feel the feelings knowing that you will recover by doing so.

My Thoughts on Avoidance Behaviour

Avoidance is probably the most common safety behaviour to manage or cope with anxiety. This is because avoiding situations that are causing anxiety seems like the sensible thing to do, even when our anxiety subsides and we want to ensure it doesn't return.

Conversely, although we believe avoiding people, places, and situations helps, it actually does the opposite. It feeds and strengthens the fear of anxiety and fuels it so that each time we step outside of our comfort zone, we face an exaggerated rush of it.

Another problem with using avoidance to cope with anxiety is that it expands. What I mean by this is that it may start with you avoiding one thing, but it doesn't stop there – over time, you will witness the list of things you avoid, for fear of becoming anxious, grow. In my experience, it began with avoiding public transport, and within a short time, it had escalated to all forms of transportation. And the sole reason for this is that the cause of feeling anxious is not the people, places, and situations we've associated it with. Instead, it is our thoughts and beliefs that trigger it. And this pattern of thinking will only continue to associate more and more things as time goes on. It's not anxiety that shrinks our world. It is the avoidance behaviour that does and our association with what we believe causes us anxiety.

This was a real eye-opener for me as I was someone who's number one coping method was avoidance, so much so that the very idea of doing anything different to what I was doing wasn't up for discussion.

The good news is you can break free from this unhelpful behaviour, and although, at first, it feels challenging and scary, it is also rewarding and empowering. Ironically, living life in avoidance is tricky and tiring and full of negatives, such as guilt, shame, and frustration. But the most crucial fact about living in avoidance is that it will never bring you the freedom you crave.

I want to stress here that I'm nothing special. I was just someone who desperately wanted their freedom back. Finally, I'd become so tired of living a life of restrictions, controlled by my thoughts and anxious feelings, that I was willing to take the risk and do anything to find freedom from anxiety.

Here's the thing. If you don't take action, you will remain stuck and feel discomfort and suffering. If you do act, you will initially experience some discomfort but it won't be the suffering kind. It somehow feels different because you know it's leading to freedom.

The thing to remember is that avoidance strengthens fear and fuels anxiety: that is all it does. It doesn't keep you safe (you aren't actually in danger when you are in fear of anxiety), and it keeps you stuck in an anxious cycle while shrinking your world. To break this cycle, you must stop avoiding things and start showing the brain that you don't need protecting. Because the brain takes time to unlearn your fear you will need to do it repeatedly before it believes you and stops reacting as if you are in danger. But if you want to overcome your fear of anxiety and get your life back you need to do the thing you feared as often as you can.

You Can't Think Your Way Out of Anxiety

Here's something to remember about anxiety. More often than not, we try to think our way out of it, which is impossible to do. Why?

Because we will almost always become entangled in the mind's fear-based thoughts and negative stories, which will stimulate the anxious mind and produce even more anxiety.

Here's some wisdom a Buddhist monk gave me at one of the mindfulness sessions I attended: the best thing to do when feeling anxious is to get out of your head and back into the present moment. They also said, 'Lisa, become the action taker, not the worrier!' Why did they say this is the best thing to do? Because an anxious mind is like an internet troll. It talks all kinds of nonsense and untruths that don't deserve your attention, and the more you engage with it, the louder and more persistent it becomes. The uncomfortable feelings you experience while engaging in these thoughts is the fear response reacting to your attention to these thoughts and how they make you feel.

This resonated with me so much because of all the hours, weeks, months, and even years I'd spent worrying. Yet, I never found any rational, soothing, or empowering guidance I desperately needed and searched for. An anxious mind will never tell you that you are safe or offer you the slightest bit of comfort.

However, we continue to make this mistake because we believe we will find a way out of feeling anxiety somewhere in our minds. But, unfortunately, we never will. The more we engage with the anxious mind, the more scaremongering it creates. Knowing and accepting this helped me to stop worrying and sitting in my thoughts.

Another trick that helped me break this cycle and stop myself from slipping down the rabbit hole was journaling about my fears. I would write them down and then pull on the evidence of why what the mind was saying was nonsense. I also started doing the opposite of what my thoughts suggested because this was a guaranteed way to prove that the anxious mind lies and tricks you. I basically stopped relying on my thoughts as a guide when I was anxious and recognised them as the fuel that would only exaggerate and make my anxiety and worrying worse.

Doing something you thought you couldn't because of anxiety is another excellent way to break the cycle of overthinking stuff and make a commitment to yourself never to allow the anxious mind to dictate or guide you through life anymore! This could range from something in everyday life such as going to a coffee morning to something as monumental as flying to a country to help run a wellbeing retreat (which I made myself do during my recovery).

Remember that the 'real you' is still there underneath the fear and anxiety. You're not lost. You're just experiencing inner turbulence and unhelpful thinking habits that will fade and pass much quicker if you stop giving them your attention!

Remind yourself how you've dealt with every anxious moment you've ever experienced up until now. Acknowledge that by developing an 'I can do this!' mindset rather than listening to your anxious thoughts and trying to think your way out of anxiety, it will significantly serve you in your recovery!

Everyone Should Have Therapy

Yes, but let's be realistic here, not everyone can have therapy because of the lack of accessibility to free treatment and the high fees to go private. People don't avoid reaching out and getting help solely because of mental health stigma. They also don't get the help they need because they are on a long NHS waiting list, or it's just too expensive to go private.

I am not begrudging anyone who earns a living from private therapy. I am saying that because mental health practices outside of the private sector are limited and in desperate need of improvement in their quality and accessibility, people who are not financially able to pay for private treatment have limited options available. It's a tough one.

I have experienced sessions with both NHS and private therapists over the years. Unfortunately, my experience with the NHS was pointless because they were extremely textbook led, asking me the same thing repeatedly and giving a brief explanation of the homework handout they passed me to look at in my own time. There was never anything to challenge me or dig deeper into my beliefs, just the weekly questionnaire to see if I was suicidal or not and the 'How are you doing?' where I would describe my week, and that was it. It lacked structure and meaning, in my opinion. I thought therapy would guide me through recovery, but after the sixth session, I'd always feel like I would have to figure it out for myself if I were ever to recover.

In all honesty, the sessions I had privately, which I had high hopes for, were very similar to the NHS ones, but the therapist would 'clock watch' (to make sure I didn't get any more than I paid for, I'm guessing). The clock watching would put me right off, and I'd end up feeling deflated because I'd spent good money to get expert advice to help me recover, only to be left feeling ripped off and let down.

I am not alone in this either. I have spoken with many people who have had similar experiences over the years. So it is no wonder people get fed up with hearing 'get help' because it is not always that simple for the reasons I have mentioned above. While I don't know what the answer is to solve the

NHS mental health crisis, I will say that I really benefited from incorporating some self-help alongside seeing a therapist. I reached a point where all they could offer was CBT, and I just knew that wasn't enough. By then, I'd gained so much knowledge from my own research into anxiety I felt empowered enough to put what I'd learnt into practice. This was when I truly reached a holistic approach to my anxiety recovery.

One thing that can help you find the right treatment is: when you receive a diagnosis from your doctor and are referred for treatment, it's OK to ask for a therapist who specialises in what you are suffering with to provide that treatment. And if you are going private, do your research, or even better, only go to a therapist you've received a recommendation for by someone you know and trust. Just because a therapist has letters after their name does not mean they are a good therapist for you or specialise in what you are experiencing. And if you are looking for a therapist on social media, be mindful that anyone can portray themselves as an expert on there. When a therapist is claiming they are 'THE BEST' and their fees reflect that, do your research, and look for the hard evidence to confirm before parting with your money.

I have written this chapter because I know first-hand how hard it can be to find the right treatment and a good therapist. You can easily end up going from one let down to another if you're not careful, which is why I opted for Dr Weekes (via her books) in the end, as she was the only one that I resonated with and whose words both comforted and empowered me to recover. I also want you to know that this is a problem across the globe, so you are not alone if you too have struggled with finding a good source for therapy.

Furthermore, I want to add that since recovering from anxiety and seeing the need for more profound healing surrounding my self-worth and trauma, I have found some beautiful therapists online who have helped me with this. After chatting with them and acknowledging how they made me feel, I researched them and decided that they were a good fit for me. That would be one of my tips: see if you can talk to a therapist before you even book a session with them and trust your gut.

So, should everyone have therapy? Well, in an ideal world I guess it could be beneficial, but only if it serves you in a way that you see results and for as long as it is helpful. I am a true believer that learning to become your own source of support is one of the best life skills you can achieve.

CHAPTER SEVEN

Soothing and Grounding Techniques That Helped Me Cope with Anxiety

When I first started to recover properly, I knew there would be times when the anxiety sensations would be strong and challenging. Therefore, knowing what would help me through the difficult times was essential. But unfortunately, I was all too aware that when anxiety levels are high, it can trick you into false beliefs and stop you from thinking clearly, so to reduce that risk, I carried a list of the things I knew would soothe and help me cope when needed.

For Instant Relief

Re-labelling what was happening

I found this technique so helpful because anxiety and panic would make me feel like I was about to have a heart attack or worse. So I'd remind myself: 'I'm experiencing a surge of adrenaline, which is harmless, it's temporary, and there's nothing I need to do.' Remembering that my body is activating its fight-or-flight response (a natural threat response that's designed to keep me alive) and knowing it will pass was really grounding for me.

Grounding technique – 5, 4, 3, 2, 1

This technique takes you through your five senses to help remind you of the present. It is calming and helped me get through the tough, challenging, and anxious times.

Take a deep belly breath to begin.

5. SEE: Look around for five things you can see and say them aloud.

4. FEEL: Touch or feel four things and say them aloud, e.g. the bark of a tree, your feet in the grass, or an ice cube on your neck and wrists.

3. LISTEN: Listen for three sounds. It could be the sound of birds, traffic outside etc. Say the three things aloud.

2. SMELL: Notice two things you can smell. And say them aloud.

1. TASTE: Taste something and say what it is out loud. It may be a mint or a drink. If you can't taste anything, say your favourite thing to taste. I would always sip iced cold water for this.

Don't rush through this exercise. Instead, take your time really focusing on the senses as you go through them.

Box or square breathing technique

Look for a square object (anything as long as it is square) and focus on the top left-hand corner. Take a slow deep breath in for four while tracing your eyes across to the right-hand corner. Hold that breath for four while tracing your eyes down to the bottom right-hand corner. Exhale for four while tracing your eyes across to the bottom left-hand corner and inhale for four as you return to the top left-hand side.

This technique is about inhaling for four, holding for four, and exhaling for four while using the square shape as a guide to keep your attention on your breathing. Keep going until you feel yourself calming, which you will. I would make sure I practised this and other breathing exercises when I wasn't anxious because it is so good for you.

Movement

With all the adrenaline in your system it is helpful to move as this burns the adrenaline off. Walking was my thing as well as dancing (when at home). Although I had to let go of resisting the anxious feelings to recover fully, I found moving in any way rather than sitting and allowing myself to focus on the anxious thoughts really helped me to resist the anxious feelings.

Music

This goes without saying and never fails to soothe me. I used music as a form of prevention and a way to reduce my anxiety levels.

Talking

I know it is not for everyone but for me it helped, especially when feeling overwhelmed. Talking it through with a therapist or someone I knew would understand how I was feeling always helped.

Listening

When I felt restless, I'd listen to music or an inspiring podcast or audiobook. I found these would gently shift my attention away from my thoughts and help me feel more relaxed.

Kundalini yoga

This yoga practice is all about the breath, so I found it incredibly helpful with my anxiety, especially when suffering from GAD.

Being in nature

Nature, without a doubt, was one of the tools I used more frequently than anything else to recover. Whether it was sitting in the garden, doing some gardening, or going for a walk in the countryside, it really did heal and calm me.

Journaling

This helped me reduce any stress and anxiety by serving as a way to escape and release my negative thoughts and feelings. It also helped me process and understand my emotions better. I find journaling helpful and an excellent way to clear my head.

I imagine you've heard of most (if not all) of the above as great tools to help reduce anxiety. Yet we struggle to do them, right? But the one thing I have learnt through my own experience is that you cannot recover from anxiety if you continue to do the very things that are causing or stimulating it. Having strategies to cope helped me become more resilient and made it easier to adapt to my new healthy way of responding to anxiety. However, these only worked once I had identified the main source of my anxiety and managed to remove anything from my life that was fuelling my anxiety.

How I Cope and Deal with Anxious Thoughts Today

I still get times when my head fills up with anxious thoughts, usually when I am doing something new or am feeling low. I believe this is completely normal for us humans and is part of brain activity.

Before I recovered, anxious thoughts seemed like the only thinking going on in my brain. I couldn't seem to break free of the endless fear-mongering and worst-case scenarios my brain produced.

It was only after hearing phrases like 'Thoughts Are Not Facts' and 'You Are the Observer of Your Thoughts' I started to learn that thought is neutral, neither good nor bad; it is our perception of the thought that categorises it. I was blown away by this because up until then (almost 13 years into my anxiety struggles) no one had ever shared this information. Not doctors or therapists. It was all new to me.

I learnt that thoughts are a mixture of predictions, assumptions, stories, beliefs, and memories. They are the brain's data that it repeatedly regurgitates depending on the trigger and situation. They are trying to help you understand what's going on around you, but they are not facts.

It took me a long time to understand all this information. Finally, by reading books from geniuses like Eckart Tolle and Michael Singer, I learnt more about how the mind works, mainly how thoughts work.

The key is to distance yourself from anxious thoughts, become the observer, and not willingly engage with them. Also, stop trying to get rid of them because as much as we don't want these kinds of thoughts, we cannot simply rid ourselves of them. Trust me; it takes practice.

Mindfulness

This is a is powerful tool for practising how to not engage with anxious thoughts. I started to attend the local Buddhist Centre's weekly classes to learn from the masters of mindfulness. It helped me so much, plus I got to pick the monks' brains for more mind-calming tips.

Re-labelling my anxious thoughts

With time and work, this became a skill I learnt and started to use. I named them my 'nonsense' thoughts, and when they appeared, I would say to myself, 'Oh, these are my nonsense thoughts, they are not valid, and I don't need to engage with them or give them any meaning.' I would also acknowledge that the brain was offering up these 'nonsense' thoughts as an automated response because I was feeling low or doing something new.

Challenging my anxious thoughts

Another successful method I used to help soothe myself. First, I would write down exactly what my anxious thoughts were followed by any evidence that proved them to be true. Then, I would write down any evidence that disproved them. I found this exercise so helpful. But again, it takes time to dismantle our belief in these anxious thoughts. Also, be mindful that the mind will come up with false evidence to support the anxious thoughts, so you need to be completely honest while considering the evidence.

Shifting my focus

This proved extremely helpful. For example, when my mind began to fill up with anxious thoughts (this happened a lot in the mornings), I would remind myself that when I focus on them, I slip down the rabbit hole of doom, and my body responds with anxiety. Then I'd ask myself, do I want that? I found giving myself a choice helped break the momentum of the thoughts.

I'd remind myself that you can't get rid of thoughts, so there is no point in becoming tangled up in them by trying, as this will only exaggerate them. The best thing to do is to carry on with my day, which will quieten them quicker.

These practices I did took time and effort to really start working and even now I have to really focus on what I'm doing if they're going to work. They are not an instant fix, as I found nothing is when it comes to an anxious mind. But over time, they will form a new habit in how you cope with anxious thoughts.

CHAPTER EIGHT

My Hero, Dr Claire Weekes

I couldn't write a book without including a chapter on my hero, lifesaver, and recovery guide, Dr Claire Weekes, because it was her books that led me to recovery. I am happy to confirm that I had permission from Dr Weekes's family to include this chapter in my book.

What we now call anxiety disorder is what Dr Weekes called 'nervous illness'.

It's crucial you know this because you'll find her books use some wording that we don't use today. But please don't let that put you off. For example, one word she uses a lot is 'accepting'. Today, you'll find the word 'surrender', 'allow', or 'wilful tolerance' used by others, but it means the same thing – 'accept.' The principles are almost identical. I discovered from reading her books that Dr Weekes was undoubtedly the pioneering leader in anxiety recovery. For me, she was the answer to my prayers and the guiding light to freedom away from an unhealthy and disordered relationship with anxiety.

What I Learnt from Dr Weekes

Much of the following advice and quotes are from Dr Weekes's first book, *Self Help for Your Nerves*. (Titled *Hope and Help for your Nerves* in the USA)

'I am not broken'

Like so many, I believed that anxiety was a bad thing. Something that I needed to suppress or run away from. Dr Weekes taught me otherwise. Her books explain how anxiety is a natural function of the nervous system and not some inherent flaw. And when the nervous system is continuously activated/sensitised, it will produce intense and scary bodily symptoms. She calls this, 'a state in which nerves are conditioned to react to stress in an exaggerated way; that is, they bring unusually intense feelings when under stress, and at times with alarming swiftness.' And these high levels of sensitisation can lead to the negative symptoms we experience with anxiety, just like the kind of symptoms I have mentioned in this book.

These symptoms and sensations make us think we are in imminent physical danger. And because we don't have an accurate or educated understanding of anxiety, we suppress, struggle, and fight it, leading to more sensitivity. This cycle is what we call an anxiety disorder, and it continues until we stop fighting and learn not to fear it. This information was a game-changer and helped me squash the fears I had carried around for years.

'Face, accept, float, and let time pass'

Dr Weekes explains how people need to face the anxiety to break the cycle and allow it to pass. Her method is to acknowledge the sensations, but instead of running away or trying to suppress them, you should accept what is taking place. However, she also says that it is necessary to make sure that the anxiety is not crippling. From this advice, I took action to reduce my anxiety levels to a more manageable level before attempting her method.

Mind you, even when my anxiety was at an all-time high, engulfing me in continuous fear, I would listen to Dr Weekes's audios to let her words sink in to offer reassurance and build my knowledge on what to do once my anxiety was at a more manageable level. I would repeatedly listen to the part where she explained the 'Accept, Float, and Let Time Pass' approach so that I knew the ins and outs before giving it a go. It helped so much because I found her words so empowering. After all, even though I knew facing my fears would be challenging, her words reassured me that I was not in any danger whatsoever.

'Take my time and be patient'

The recovery process can be long and exhausting. At times, I became so frustrated and impatient that I'd find myself doubting the process and looking for those quick fixes all over again. Dr Weekes names this 'bewilderment', where we become impatient. I experienced this where doubt would kick in, and I'd panic about the symptoms all over again. However, her explanation of this happening was also a comfort. She advises that the key to recovery is to remain patient.

Setbacks are further opportunities for me to cement what I've learnt

Dr Weekes taught me that setbacks didn't mean I had gone back to square one. Instead, they are part of the recovery process, and we should never deter from learning from them. Dr Weekes helped me believe that I was stronger and more capable than my years of suffering had led me to believe. This was a crucial turning point in my recovery. I began seeing beyond my anxious thoughts about anxiety, which shifted my perception of my ability to recover and get my life back on track.

I will be forever grateful that Dr Weekes came to the forefront with her beliefs on anxiety recovery and published her books. To this day, I see her work changing people's lives. However, I believe that there is no 'one-way suits all' method for anxiety recovery. But I have to admit, I think the Dr Weekes method comes pretty close!

Dr Weekes's Published Works

Self Help for Your Nerves (1962) (sold over 300,000 copies and translated into eight languages)

Then renamed *Hope and Help for Your Nerves* and published in America (1969)

Peace from Nervous Suffering (1972)

Simple, Effective Treatment of Agoraphobia (1976)

More Help for Your Nerves (1984)

The Latest Help for Your Nerves (1989)

Complete Self Help for Your Nerves (1997) (A compilation of *Self Help for Your Nerves* and *More Help for Your Nerves*)

Essential Help for Your Nerves (2000) (comprises two books: *More Help for Your Nerves* and *Peace from Nervous Suffering*)

Alternative versions:

In 1983, Dr Weekes gave a series of short interviews called 'Peace from Nervous Suffering' – available on Apple TV.

Audio recordings of *Hope and Help for Your Nerves* and *Freedom from Nervous Suffering* can be found through Audible, Amazon or other online providers.

You can also follow her works through the Instagram page set up by her family: @claireweekespublications.

CHAPTER NINE

My Experience with Medication

Because of all the stigma and pill shaming going around about people who take medication I just had to share my experience. Taking medication for anxiety is perfectly OK, as is not taking medication if you don't want to. What isn't OK is people who belittle and shame others who do. I have experienced first-hand the 'pill shaming' and, at times, felt the guilt and embarrassment that comes with it.

Medication is a personal choice that should be respected and not something to feel guilty about. If you take meds, it is not a sign of weakness, nor is it defeating the object of recovery. On the contrary, medication can play a positive part in recovery if combined with therapy and a doctor monitoring the situation.

Medication isn't a cure for anxiety; it only masks and eases the symptoms. This certainly appeared to be why I was offered them in the early 1990s; it seemed as if it was the only option. There was no offer of CBT or information about recovery. At times, I was keen to come off the medication, but soon after my symptoms would re-occur. What I've since learnt is that medication can provide you with the breathing space you may desperately need to do therapy effectively. I've been on and off anti-depressants for over 27 years, but they are used in combination with other forms of therapy.

Thankfully, things are different now and people are given a choice regarding how they want to manage their anxiety and recover. Ultimately, I don't think either way is terrible. It again boils down to what feels good to you.

In my case, the inability to eat was one symptom I struggled with each time my anxiety soared. And this would cause drastic weight loss and extreme weakness. However, after trying numerous things to help me overcome this, things only improved when I went back on the medication. Here, I want to stress the importance of acknowledging how anxiety can affect people differently. In addition, the severity of symptoms can differ, so for some, medication can be a lifesaver and not something to be frowned on. For others, they feel they can recover without medication, which is also a personal choice.

We need to stop thinking that just because one person overcame anxiety without medication then everyone should. Instead, we need to accept that people are different. For example, some people can work with a bad cold, while others can't. Some people get over a virus quite quickly and others don't. We are the same because we are all human, but we are also different in many ways, especially when healing and recovering from things.

There is also the stigma and fear surrounding withdrawal from anti-depressants. Well, in my experience, I have known people who have been on medication for a long time come off them with very little to no withdrawal symptoms while others had a struggle. I tried several times without success, but this was my own experience and shouldn't set a precedent. The first time I tried coming off my medication, I had been using my meds for 15 years. Up until that point, my doctor had told me that I needed to stay on them for the rest of my life. Even though my recovery hadn't even started, the stigma surrounding taking anti-depressants pushed me into trying to come off them. So when I tried, I had intense withdrawal symptoms, meaning I'd restart them.

My experience with coming off medication combined with being a single parent were significant factors in deciding to stay on the medication. As the only breadwinner, staying well was paramount, meaning I couldn't afford to fall ill while attempting to withdraw from medication.

In my experience, people don't take medication because they are weak or too lazy to go through the hard stuff to recover without help. Instead, it comes down to a combination of factors: their situation, the severity of their symptoms, and after a discussion with their doctor. I believe it isn't an easy decision either, but it may be a much better option than feeling that suicide is the only way to stop the horror they are going through.

Anxiety affects people differently, so it only makes sense that how people manage anxiety and recover will differ.

FAQs on Medication

Do I think it is OK to take medication?

It is a personal choice and one you should discuss with your doctor. But I do believe it is not a sign of weakness or should be viewed as a negative thing.

Do meds help with my anxiety?

Yes. They are not a cure but instead ease my symptoms enough to provide some much-needed breathing space to aid my recovery.

Did I do therapy while on medication?

I did all my CBT, exposure therapy, and self-help while on medication. I was still able to experience some fear and panic, which I believe I needed to feel to recovered.

Does medication make me feel like a zombie?

Not at all, quite the opposite. It puts a spring back in my step. I hear some say theirs made them feel numb, but I have never experienced anything like that. I am able to feel love, have sex, cry, laugh; all the things I felt prior to suffering from anxiety.

Why have I taken medication for so long?

My initial prognosis was that I would suffer with anxiety forever and so needed to stay on the tablets. (It was the 1990s and seemed to be the common prognosis in the UK back then.) At that point I didn't know any different. I had already been on them for 15 years before finding out that I could recover and not need them forever. But by then I'd been on them for a long time and to be honest I was too scared to stop taking them. Life is good now and I don't want to rock the boat.

Do I have any side effects?

Only when I miss a few doses, because the medication I am on means when you miss just a couple of doses you can feel the effects almost immediately. I can start to feel woozy and experience 'brain zaps'. But as soon as I take one that stops.

Would I recommend taking medication for anxiety?

I would recommend always talking to your doctor about what your options are when struggling with anxiety. That is what I did and for me medication helped no end.

Do I wish I wasn't on medication?

Maybe. But not if it meant me going back to how I was before, and to be honest, right now, I wouldn't want to take the risk. However, when I was first prescribed them, I wish I'd used them how they should be used; combined with therapy. But eventually, that is what I did, and I have no regrets.

One thing I no longer do is beat myself up over it... and nor should you.

CHAPTER TEN

The Power of Being Patient

This short chapter must be the most important one I've written for this book because when we become impatient in recovery, we risk undoing all the hard work. Impatience is something I struggled with at the start of my recovery. I just wanted to feel normal NOW. I'd spent years suffering, and now that I had finally found the way to recover in Dr Weekes's books, I wanted it to happen immediately.

I kept dismissing any advice I was given to 'slow down... accept and trust the process', which allowed self-doubt to creep back in because I wasn't seeing my progress quickly enough. I guess I still had the idea of a quick fix in the back of my mind. If you are feeling like this: trust me, I get it!

But the thing is, being impatient doesn't benefit the healing process or you in any way. The only thing it leads to is a sense of frustration and helplessness. I now realise how closely anxiety and impatience are linked: waiting for relief feels even harder when suffering.

To help me with this, my father told me to see my recovery like an athlete sees an injury. The athlete is desperate to get back to training but realises that this would only hinder the healing process and possibly cause further injury. My anxiety recovery was the same. I had to learn to be patient because my impatience would only aggravate the anxiety, cause me further stress, and possibly prolong or hinder the recovery process. Also, when you become impatient, you tend to focus ONLY on the negatives of a situation and end up thinking stuff like 'this isn't going to work for me', instead of saying to yourself, 'I'm healing and working through my recovery. It may take a bit of time, but that's OK!'

The best thing I did was accept that anxiety recovery takes time. Suppose you're having therapy or following someone qualified – like I did with Dr Weekes's guidance. Listen closely to what they suggest. I bet you somewhere they will stress the importance of being patient. Yes, you must do the work but go at a sensible pace, remove all expectations, and shower yourself with kindness and compassion, being proud of every step you take, no matter how small. Please don't allow the urgency to heal ruin your progress.

Remember, impatience takes up so much mental energy but doesn't change or improve anything. All it does is add to your suffering and hinder recovery. So, wherever you are on your path to recovery, please be patient with yourself. No matter how slow it may seem right now, you are heading in the right direction. So do not lose hope.

Learning to be patient was the best thing I did for my recovery.

CHAPTER ELEVEN

Posts from My

@SIMPLY_ANXIOUS

Instagram Page

I SEE YOU

Anxiety isn't just about feeling scared, agitated, and shaky... It's about waking up at 3am night after night to a barrage of debilitating fear, after spending hours desperately trying to fall asleep.

It's about the pain I felt as I watched the job opportunities, social events, holidays, relationships, and friendships slip through my fingers. It's about the stigma I experienced and derogatory comments.

It's about periods spent yearning for validation, understanding and reassurance that I'll be OK. It's about the self-loathing I felt because anxiety made me feel like a burden.

It's about spending all my time googling symptoms, scrolling endlessly through anxiety forums and social media pages just hoping something somewhere will take away the fear.

It's about finally sitting in a therapy session full of hope. But the therapist keeps clock watching which ruins the experience and makes me feel like a statistic.

It's about questioning how I got here over and over again while crying painful tears at what feels like the loss of the person I once was. It's about wondering how long I can do this.

It's about trying to come up with excuses of why I yet again can't go somewhere that won't upset my family or friends. It's about the fear people will give up on me. It's about the loneliness I feel but also the need to be alone because it feels safer.

It's about spending hours considering whether to take the diazepam prescribed by my doctor for emergencies when anxiety is so bad but being too scared to take it for fear it will make me feel worse. It's about calling my doctor and have them sit on the phone while I take a pill to help settle my nerves.

It's about pacing around the house while everyone sleeps trying to find a sense of safety. It's about feeling incredibly isolated even in a house full of people. It's about being hugged for reassurance and feeling nothing.

This post is about the not so talked about things people experience while battling with anxiety.

Lisa x

ANXIETY QUOTE: I WISH I HAD

I WISH I HAD CONTROL OVER
THESE PANIC ATTACKS. BUT
AS ANYONE WITH ANXIETY
UNDERSTANDS, SOMETIMES
YOU CAN ONLY OPERATE ON
ITS TERMS!
ARIANA GRANDE

@SIMPLY_ANXIOUS

There will be periods where anxiety is so overwhelming that everything you thought you knew about anxiety and any progress made in your recovery will seem like it's vanished. But that is not true because it hasn't!

This very fear is a common symptom of overwhelm, exhaustion and is part of the healing process. Recovery is about creating a new understanding and relationship with anxiety, knowing no matter how bad it feels, it WILL pass and refraining from any struggle will allow that to happen quicker.

While recovering, you don't have to force yourself to do things and battle through every day. Instead, allow yourself to go at your own pace and accept what comes up. There will be days you can go at it head-on, push your boundaries and do the things you thought you couldn't. And then there will be days where all you want to do is 'nothing', and those days are equally as important for recovery. Remember, people who don't struggle with anxiety have bad days too.

There is only one rule in recovery: to do what is best for you at any given moment. Knowing you have this control can only be a good thing and a benefit to you.

THOUGHTS ARE NOT FACTS

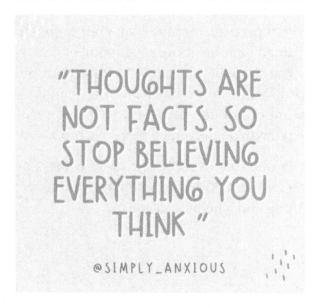

"THOUGHTS ARE NOT FACTS. SO STOP BELIEVING EVERYTHING YOU THINK "

@SIMPLY_ANXIOUS

Honestly, the worst thing you can do when feeling anxious is to listen to your anxious thoughts!

An anxious mind categorically lies and does it so convincingly that it will almost always leave you in a total meltdown.

The ones I had were relentless and kept me locked in anxious mode 24/7. But why did I believe them for so long? Because no one had ever told me that thoughts (especially anxious ones) are not facts. Who knew, right?

I also had no idea that anxiety was a harmless human emotion that could become challenging when misunderstood and feared. Or, come to think of it, how highly treatable anxiety is. So, excuse me for behaving in a way that innocently fuelled anxiety for many years.

But once I did get this valuable information, I didn't sit on it. Instead, I used it to my advantage. I began challenging my anxious thoughts by writing them down and then writing the facts next to them like in the slides. I started practising doing the opposite of what they told me. And I labelled them as nonsense and stopped identifying with them. All this took time and practice, but it's what eventually exposed the lies and tricks the anxious mind tells. And for recovery, this is powerful!

See if you can see the kind of lies your anxious mind has told you. And let's see if you can prove them wrong.

WHAT 20 YEARS OF SUFFERING FROM ANXIETY LOOKED LIKE FOR ME

Anxiety Recovery –

WHAT 20 YEARS OF SUFFERING FROM ANXIETY LOOKED LIKE

I would go through different stages of anxiety. They were:

Chronic anxiety

High functioning anxiety

GAD

And what I call – Dormant anxiety

@simply_anxious

I often post about how exposure therapy helped me recover, and that's true.

But reassurance, soothing, medication, time out, and self-help did too.

There will be times when you need soothing and other times when all you need is a push. For example, when I was experiencing periods of chronic anxiety, there was absolutely no way on earth I could have attempted exposure therapy because I could barely function doing anything. What I needed in those times was reassurance, comfort and soothing to reduce my anxiety levels. So, in those periods of chronic anxiety, I opted for medication to help me. And after a few months, I felt more able to take more active steps to combat my fear with the proper support and guidance.

Anxiety Recovery – CHRONIC ANXIETY

How it felt	How I coped with it
Like I was stuck in a huge cloud of intense fear and unable to do anything like shower, watch tv, eat	Reached out for reassurance and support
	I'd drink lots of water
Derealisation, my hearing went muffled and my sight fuzzy and I had no sense of being	Played nature sounds and soothing music on loop, listened to inspiring audio books
Trembles, that made me feel like every cell in my body was frazzled and wired	Talk over things with people I trust and the doctor
Intense sense of doom, sometimes suicidal thoughts,	Allow myself time and space to just be
	Took medication

@simply_anxious

In GAD and high-functioning anxiety, I would feel anxious but try to carry on regardless by using unhealthy coping methods like drinking and overworking. Not a smart move, but at the time, I was hoping anxiety would give up the chase and disappear on its own. But unfortunately, that doesn't happen. So here I needed to take time out and own my recovery by making some lifestyle changes, putting my energy into facing my fears, and dismantling my safety behaviours.

Anxiety Recovery –
GENERALISED ANXIETY (GAD)

How it felt

Like every nerve in my body was wired and my senses heightened

Racing thoughts and troublesome physical symptoms e.g tight painful neck, shoulders and tension headaches

Frequent anxiety attacks through the day and night (not panic attacks)

How I coped with it

Stayed hydrated and drank smoothies (struggled to eat)

Sought help from a therapist

Did Kundalini Yoga lessons (great for anxiety)

Daily short walks

Reading or listening to self help inspiring books

Talked with those close to me or like-minded people

@simply_anxious

Anxiety Recovery –
HIGH FUNCTIONING ANXIETY

How it felt	How I stopped doing this
Like I was running a marathon daily	Accepted I needed help
Like I had to keep pushing myself because if I stopped I'd fall apart	Reached out for support and opened up about my struggle
Like I had to self medicate with alcohol to be able to sleep	Took time out, time off work etc
Like I was a walking time bomb	Cut out the booze and started going to a Buddhist centre to learn about the mind and ways to calm it
Exhausting	Started therapy

@simply_anxious

The dormant anxiety was where I didn't experience anxiety that much, but my fear of it remained. These periods were short-lived. They occurred when I became deeply involved in something, e.g., a work project or something that took up all my attention. But there was always a part of me fearing anxiety's return, so avoidance was still my number one coping behaviour which, of course, kept anxiety simmering away in the background.

Anxiety Recovery –
DORMANT ANXIETY

How it felt	How I finally stopped doing this
Like I was on the look out 24/7	Made a commitment to work on my recovery properly once and for all
Unable to relax or let my hair down	Did CBT and exposure therapy
Like I had to plan and micromanage everything I did to stop anxiety showing up	Continued exposure therapy with the help of Dr Claire Weekes and Paul David
Restrictive and joyless	Started raising awareness of anxiety
Exhausting	Made a few lifestyle changes that supported my recovery

@simply_anxious

Anxiety can have different intensity levels, so combining different healing approaches is more effective than the 'one-way suits all' approach.

I'M NOT FAKING BEING SICK

I'M NOT FAKING
BEING SICK.
I'M ACTUALLY
FAKING BEING
WELL

@SIMPLY_ANXIOUS

I remember times when I was crumbling inside, gasping for air, screaming out for help only to be met by people looking at me with confused faces and dismissal. Telling me to 'get a grip' and 'not be stupid' only made my struggle with anxiety more challenging. Since then, a lot has changed regarding mental health, but it still needs work.

If you're struggling, I want you to know that you don't need to feel ashamed, you're human, and humans have brains. Brains get tired, overwhelmed, and stressed, just like limbs and other parts of the body. The only difference between mental health struggles and physical health struggles is the stigma developed through ignorance and lack of education. But it seems that society is waking up and taking this much more seriously, which is a good thing.

Please, don't feel embarrassed or ashamed. Don't brush aside your struggle because of what other people might say. Express how you feel. Accept your emotions and face whatever is causing them. Acknowledge those emotions and seek help if you need it. Trust me, even if your feelings seem irrational, unreasonable, or extreme, they are not.

You do not have to suppress your emotions anymore. Your feelings matter. Your feelings are valid and there is help and support out there, so please reach out. □

OVERTHINKING

"OVERTHINKING:
THE ART OF
CREATING
PROBLEMS THAT
WEREN'T EVEN
THERE. "

@SIMPLY_ANXIOUS

Overthinking must be up there as one of the most annoying, self-defeating, and time-consuming behaviours we do. And it gets us nowhere!

But we know that, right? And yet we still do it!

We overthink because we/the mind loves certainty and to feel in control. It's part of our human survival tactic. The problem is that the more we overthink, the more fear we invite in and the more intrusive or anxious our thoughts become. It's a vicious cycle, especially for those who suffer from anxiety.

Overthinking is not the same as planning or problem-solving. It would be more accurate to name it 'problem-creating' because it comes from fear. So, overthinking will only produce scary worst-case scenario thoughts and not thoughts about success or enjoyment. So, if you catch yourself falling into the overthinking mode, remind yourself of this!

Here's a trick I use when I feel myself slipping into the land of overthinking. I recognise what I'm doing (grab that awareness) and ask myself, "why do I need to know?" and "there is no way of knowing until I experience it for myself."

If it is persistent, I start singing or talking as these release stress and help shift my attention.

The thing is, NO amount of time spent overthinking will convince you of a positive outcome, but taking action, talking, or singing will!

SOME THINGS I LEARNT

Anxiety Recovery –
SOME KEY THINGS I LEARNED!

Avoidance	Exposure
Keeps you stuck and strengthens your fear	Brings results
Tricks you into feeling a false sense of security	Provides opportunities to see how anxiety can't hurt you
Shrinks your world and stops you enjoying things	Builds self-confidence and self worth
Feeds self-doubt and the belief that you'll never overcome anxiety	Your world begins to expand and you begin to enjoy life
	Leads to recovery

@simply_anxious

I wanted to share my experience living as someone whose go-to method to cope with anxiety was avoidance for many years. And what I experienced after taking a leap of faith and doing the exposure therapy to finally overcome my fear of anxiety.

I thought it would be helpful to share what I gained from finding the courage to get help, support and do the work needed to get me out of my anxious prison.

~ 119 ~

Taking the steps needed to overcome anxiety is challenging, tiring and scary, and it's also rewarding and empowering. And let's face it, living in avoidance is also scary, challenging and tiring but will never lead you to feel rewarded or empowered.

You may not see this yet, but once you start changing how you see and react to anxiety, you will!

I realised anxiety wouldn't go away without my help and decided it was worth experiencing the discomfort if it led to my recovery. I had nearly 15 years of fearing what my thoughts suggested would happen but never actually did and years white-knuckling, avoiding, and rushing through life to try and outrun anxiety. None of which worked.

I had nothing to lose and everything to gain. So, I worked hard, supported myself when it hurt, comforted myself when I needed it and encouraged myself by acknowledging and celebrating every step I took forward.

I'm nothing special. I'm just someone who desperately wanted my life back. I became so tired of living a life of restrictions, controlled by my thoughts, and suffering as a result.

I hope you can relate, and this inspires you to start believing in yourself. Because you can overcome anxiety, just like I did. You just need to be willing to do whatever it takes □

THINGS THAT DON'T HELP ANXIETY RECOVERY

THINGS THAT 'REALLY' DON'T HELP ANXIETY RECOVERY

Being or feeling pressurised into doing things

simply_anxious ♡

I learnt very quickly that to recover from anxiety, you must want to do the things that will help you overcome your fear. You must be willing to feel the discomfort and stay with it until it subsides. I tried so many times, but the one key ingredient that was missing was that I wasn't willing to let go of resistance and sit with the discomfort.

When I felt pressurised or pushed into facing my fears, it only made me feel worse. I wasn't ready, and by that, I meant I needed time to understand how and why I was facing the fears and do some self-soothing to get my anxiety levels down to a more manageable level. It was when GAD was rife, so I didn't need to leave my house to find the fear. I was living in it 24/7. So, I needed to take teeny weeny baby steps and not the 'get yourself out there, you'll be fine' steps others wanted me to do.

We know that the only way to deal with fear is to face it, and avoiding fear prevents us from moving forward. But you must be gentle with yourself and do what feels safe to you! The more significant steps towards fear will come with time. You can't work through your recovery if you are doing it to meet the expectations of others. You must do it for yourself. You must be willing and ready, which in time you will be.

Don't compare your recovery to others or feel pressured. Instead, go at your own pace, build on your understanding, and start moving forward gently, as this will build on your 'willingness' to feel the fear and do it properly. □

ANXIETY IS NOT WHO YOU ARE

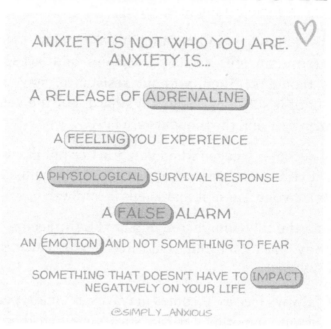

ANXIETY IS NOT WHO YOU ARE.
ANXIETY IS...

A RELEASE OF ADRENALINE

A FEELING YOU EXPERIENCE

A PHYSIOLOGICAL SURVIVAL RESPONSE

A FALSE ALARM

AN EMOTION AND NOT SOMETHING TO FEAR

SOMETHING THAT DOESN'T HAVE TO IMPACT
NEGATIVELY ON YOUR LIFE

@SIMPLY_ANXIOUS

Anxiety is something you experience. It is not who you are. It feels intense and, at times, life-threatening. It can also make you feel like you're losing your mind etc., but you're not. And it cannot hurt you.

Anxiety is a threat response that thrives off fear. However, it can trick us into fearing it, so the best way to lose that fear is to remove its cloak of uncertainty, not let it define you and take its power over you away!

Saying things like: 'I'm experiencing anxiety' rather than 'I'm going crazy and losing it' will help as it's putting truth to what's happening rather than engaging in fear-based thoughts the anxious mind is creating.

Saying the following (and meaning it!) also helps. 'I allow and accept these anxious feelings. I allow and accept these anxious thoughts.' Then, without resistance, stay with the feeling until it subsides. I know it's hard, but the sensations can't harm you, and the thoughts are false.

Anxiety becomes weaker when you practice not reacting with fear. The less you fear anxiety, the less it will show up because it's your fear of it that keeps it coming.

Try using the following acronyms for FEAR: Feeling Excited and Ready, Face Everything and Recover or False Evidence Appearing Real.

Anxiety always passes; it comes in waves; it builds, peaks, and then tails off. Sometimes it can start very quickly and fade slowly. But it always subsides.

Remind yourself that every time you've been anxious, it's passed, and the next time won't be any different. It, too, shall pass. □

SHAME

WHAT WE DON'T NEED IN THE MIDST OF STRUGGLE IS SHAME FOR BEING HUMAN.

BRENÉ BROWN

@SIMPLY_ANXIOUS

If there is one thing I urge you to do while healing anxiety, it is to lose any shame you may feel because it weighs heavily on a fearful and anxious mind.

We feel shame due to the stigma of anxiety, often seen as a negative trait, a sign of weakness and a human flaw, which is extremely ignorant of those who believe this because it is totally untrue. When I first "went public" about my struggles,

I feared that people would use it against me. But, instead, the majority began to open up about their struggles or the struggles of a loved one they wanted to support better. So, all in all, it was a positive thing.

Anxiety isn't some new mental health condition. It has always been around. It was just never talked about and instead was hidden away like a dirty little secret because of the stigma. But we don't need to hide it away or feel ashamed because there is absolutely nothing abnormal about struggling with anxiety. On the contrary, it's probably the most common symptom of stress, emotional distress, mental fatigue, unresolved trauma, etc. In the type of society we live in, it makes sense that 1 in 4 suffers. I'm a firm believer that society makes us sick and keeps us sick (because it simply doesn't allow us the time to heal).

Please don't ever feel ashamed because you have nothing to feel ashamed about. Instead, use the energy for your healing and recovery. □

ANXIETY SYMPTOMS

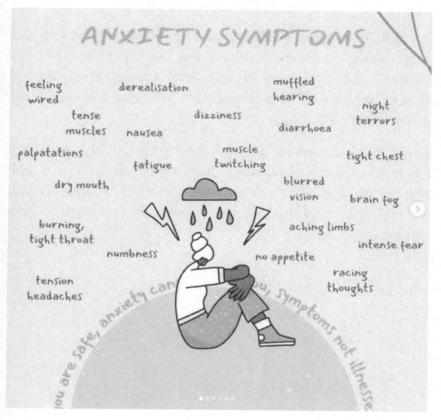

All the symptoms I mention in this post are what I experienced when battling anxiety. They would trick me into thinking time and time again that there was something seriously wrong with me!

I believed I needed medical attention or a trip to A&E. They were so convincing that even after the all-clear from a doctor,

I'd still sit worrying and overthinking them and doubting what my doctor said was the cause, 'ANXIETY!'

It's difficult as these symptoms are incredibly distressing. But don't waste your time focusing on and trying to fix them. Instead, put your energy into overcoming your fear of anxiety, which will help reduce its levels, and the symptoms will gradually disappear.

The thing to remember about symptoms is that although they can feel scary and distressing, they cannot hurt you! Just look at how many times you've experienced them, and you're still here. This is proof that you can handle any symptom anxiety throws up. □

WHY THE WORLD SHRINKS

Why does anxiety shrink your World?

With anxiety

Without anxiety

@SIMPLY_ANXIOUS ♡

It shrinks your world because you've associated the cause of your anxiety with places, things, people, and situations. But the truth is if you didn't believe that these cause your anxiety, you'd willingly do, see and try all of them.

And here's the thing. When you overcome your fear of anxiety you learn that you can cope if it shows up and it isn't something to concern yourself over. Then you will be willing to do these things and more.

Although you might feel that it's the queue in the supermarket, the traffic jam, the motorway, or the social event that's causing you anxiety, it's not. Instead, it is your thoughts and beliefs about them and your fear of feeling anxious that is

You may have experienced anxiety while doing these things before and now fear it will happen again if you return to those situations. All that's happened here is you've associated the cause of your anxiety to a thing, place, activity. I did the same thing for many years!

This association leads to avoidance behaviour, and before you know it, the world has become a much smaller place for you. Association also reinforces fear, so the brain has no other option than to accept these places and situations are a genuine threat to you.

To overcome this unhelpful pattern you need to accept that your thoughts/beliefs are causing the anxiety. Second, acknowledge you are not in any real danger, even though it may feel like you are. Remember, anxiety is a response to get you out of harm's way. It cannot hurt you!

Then gradually expose yourself to the situation while accepting the discomfort and allowing it to pass. It takes practice, so don't expect to do it once and be free. The anxiety may feel intense because the association and your fear of anxiety are strongly developed, which is OK. Stick with it, and it will get easier. Grounding and breathing techniques will help you move through this. Remember, the less you resist, the quicker the anxiety will subside.

We can experience anxiety for many reasons, but if yours is purely a result of an 'association', breaking that down will be liberating. □

I REALISED I'D STOPPED LIVING

I REALIZED TODAY THAT I HAVE STOPPED LIVING LIFE. I AM LITERALLY JUST TRYING TO GET TO THE NEXT DAY, JUST LIVING IN THE THOUGHT OF TOMORROW. I AM NOT LIVING, I AM WAITING. AND THE TROUBLE IS, I DON'T KNOW WHAT I AM EXACTLY WAITING FOR. I AM KIND OF SCARED FOR WHAT IT MIGHT BE.

@SIMPLY_ANXIOUS

I remember seeing this quote and thinking, that's me!

And in this quote lies the reason for my suffering - the words 'Living in the thought', 'Waiting' (anticipation), and 'Scared' (fear)!

I know just how difficult it is when we struggle with anxiety and feel like it has targeted us and feels so unfair! But the truth is anxiety is a natural response (albeit a scary as shit response) which only becomes a problem when we believe it is something to be feared, believe our anxious thoughts about it and try to battle with and suppress it.

When you learn to let go of your concern, resistance and fight with anxiety, it will settle back to its normal state.

You do not need to wait for something to show up that will cure you or search your anxious thoughts for a solution. These only breed fear and self-doubt.

You have everything you need inside of you to overcome your fear of anxiety, and you need to believe that because when you do, you will begin to heal and recover ☐

If for whatever reason, you don't have access to a good therapist, then Dr Claire Weekes's family have a brand new website in her honour that shares her work and wisdom - check it out because if anyone is going to guide you to recovery, it's her. www.claireweekespublications.com

JUST GET OVER IT!

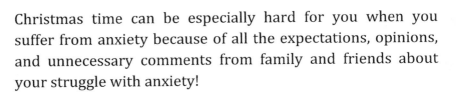

"HAVING AN ANXIETY DISORDER ISN'T EASY, AND IT'S EVEN HARDER WHEN PEOPLE ASSUME YOU CAN JUST GET OVER IT."

@SIMPLY_ANXIOUS

Christmas time can be especially hard for you when you suffer from anxiety because of all the expectations, opinions, and unnecessary comments from family and friends about your struggle with anxiety!

I would regularly get called 'Bah! Humbug!' because I wasn't filled with Christmas cheer or willing to go to the Christmas parties. Then the family meal where I'd have to sit listening to everyone's opinions about my mental health, their doubts and unhelpful advice that would make me feel worse about things.

"Get a few wines down you, and you'll be OK," "C'mon, it's Christmas, stop being silly", "Oh it's just Lisa being over dramatic as always." UFFF! No wonder I would see a decline in my mental health year after year.

Honestly, if you experience the same, please don't get sucked into it. Putting yourself and your emotional health first is so much better than trying to please those around you, trust me.

When it comes to anxiety, you can only paper over the cracks for so long until it catches up with you! Don't let this time of year force you to do that. Stand in your truth and only do what feels right for you.

To feel supported through this time of year, connect with like-minded people, spend more time in nature, get to know yourself and put your needs first. There is so much you can do to nourish and empower yourself over the holidays without having to overindulge and exhaust yourself while trying to please others☐

THE ANXIETY LOOP

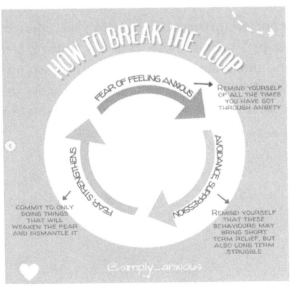

Living in an anxiety loop is not fun – once in it, you risk spending weeks, months and sometimes years just going around in circles. This fear of anxiety maintains the loop and keeps the nervous system on high alert.

I lived in this loop for a long time, all because I feared feeling anxious. All I could think about was 'not feeling anxious.' My mind became overwhelmed with trying to fix, plan and avoid anything and everything that may trigger it. I didn't understand that my not wanting to experience anxiety fuelled it and kept me stuck in the anxious cycle.

The loop strengthened each time I identified with my anxious thoughts, avoided situations, and used safety behaviours. It's a never-ending cycle unless you change how you react to anxiety.

To break the loop, I needed to stop doing all these things, especially the overanalysing and avoiding my feelings!

The best advice to break this loop is to let go of your resistance to feeling anxious. If you feel anxious, allow yourself to feel anxious. If your mind is busy, allow it to be busy. Living in this loop doesn't protect you; you don't need protection because anxiety cannot hurt you. Trying to control how you feel will only make you more vulnerable and keep you stuck.

My recovery only started when I truly accepted that I didn't have to do anything other than learn to be comfortable with the discomfort when anxious and refrain from reacting in a way that fuelled it.

The more you practice this, the less frequently anxiety will show up because this way you lose your fear of it and so no longer trigger it unnecessarily☐

GIVE YOURSELF A BREAK

Give yourself and your mind the weekend off!

Simply Anxious ♡
Helping people find freedom from anxiety

Struggling with anxiety is exhausting and can feel relentless with all that checking in, overthinking, analysing and feeling bad about yourself.

You end up spending all your time going around in circles doing the very things that keep anxiety hanging around.

As we head towards the weekend, why not try to do the opposite and give our minds a rest!

Let's stay in the NOW and allow whatever comes up to come and go by itself and let's stay disinterested.

Give it a go - you don't have to do anything. Take pleasure in knowing that you are safe and giving your overworked mind a well-deserved rest and, by doing so, allowing calmness to return. If the anxiety is a bit reluctant to settle, just allow it to have its tantrum - if you don't react, it will calm - just like a child who spits its dummy out the pram who eventually falls asleep! All your struggling, suppressing, trying to fix, overthinking and doubting hasn't helped you so far - so give yourself and the anxiety a weekend off and see how that works out! □

THE BRAIN LEARNS THROUGH REPETITION

IF SOMEONE TELLS YOU SOMETHING OVER AND OVER AGAIN YOU BEGIN TO BELIEVE IT. THAT 'SOMEONE' INCLUDES YOU...

@SIMPLY_ANXIOUS

Hands up if you negatively talk to yourself. I was terrible at it, especially while suffering from anxiety. I was always telling myself I couldn't cope or do things!

I'd say things like, 'if I do X, Y, Z, I'll definitely get anxious, make a fool of myself and cause a scene, so I best not go.' OR 'I'll never recover from anxiety because it's too powerful and I am too weak and so any effort from my side will be pointless.'

These types of inner conversations I'd frequently have with myself repeatedly. And the bizarre thing is even when life felt OK, and I was feeling calm, I would still have the 'what if' conversations going on in the background! It was as if I wasn't happy unless I was putting myself down or scaring myself silly.

Why do we do this to ourselves?

I realised that there was absolutely no way I would ever recover from anxiety if I continued to beat myself up and doubt everything. I thought about going forward. I had to learn how to stop doing this to myself.

Therapy helped. Talking about it with like-minded people also helped. I learnt to watch how I spoke to myself and started making some conscious decisions like asking myself if this conversation was supportive, empowering and, more importantly, true!

I've also learnt not to take other people's opinions of me as seriously and instead make up my mind about things. Give it a go because it's a real eye-opener to see just how easily self-limiting thoughts can suck you in and hold you back in your recovery and life in general.

IS THE PACE OF LIFE JUST TOO MUCH FOR US HUMANS?

> "MOST PEOPLE SEEM TO SUFFER FROM 'ANXIETY & DEPRESSION' THESE DAYS. IT FEELS LESS OF A 'DISORDER' AND MORE OF A NATURAL RESPONSE TO SITUATIONS THAT HUMANS AREN'T DESIGNED TO LIVE IN "
>
> @SIMPLY_ANXIOUS

In the last decade, only now have we begun to see the importance of caring for our mental health and emotional wellbeing. Society never told us the importance of that. We were taught only to 'work hard, man-up, be brave, succeed, do more, get fit, play the game, be smart, get married, have babies, honour and obey, respect your peers and work your butt off, blah blah blah...'

If we crumbled under the pressure of this blueprint, we got judged, rejected or simply left behind to fend for ourselves... No wonder there are so many of us mentally exhausted and suffering. It's exhausting trying so hard to fit into the 'how life is supposed to look and how we are supposed to be' mould while hiding our true feelings, emotions and needs!

Bit deep for a Saturday, but essential to see what's happening here. If you are struggling mentally and emotionally, it's important to know that you are not ill. Instead, you are probably mentally exhausted, emotionally confused and probably full of conflict between your true self and life's expectations.

Or maybe it's a case that you haven't been able to find the time to heal correctly from past events because life is just too damn demanding.

Do you know the old saying? If you work in a bakery, you get covered in flour. Well, if you live in an ever-demanding society, you get burnt out!

MY FAVOURITE QUOTE BY VINCENT VAN GOGH

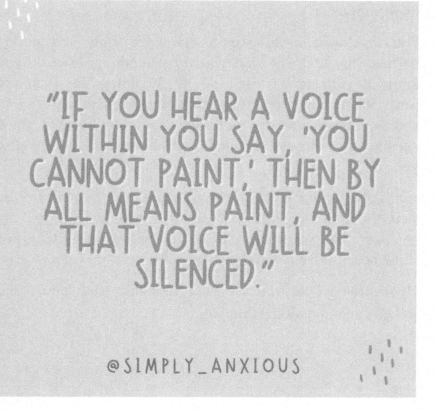

"IF YOU HEAR A VOICE WITHIN YOU SAY, 'YOU CANNOT PAINT,' THEN BY ALL MEANS PAINT, AND THAT VOICE WILL BE SILENCED."

@SIMPLY_ANXIOUS

When you listen to that voice in your head, that tells you why you can't or shouldn't do something. And you believe it. You're giving it power over you and allowing it to rob you of opportunities to prove to yourself that you can do things (even the challenging and hard things).

Instead, when you hear that voice, the one full of doubt and fear, acknowledge it, label it as untrue/nonsense, the brain's tabloid newspaper, or whatever else you want to call it and do the opposite.

You can choose not to listen to that voice or give it attention because the truth is until you try something, how do you know if you can or can't do it? By doing this, you are removing its power over you, and without that, it will pass. Of course, it takes practice, but once you get into the habit, you'll see how the voice isn't as loud or important as it once was to you.

Don't give opportunities away because of a bunch of noise that the mind produces. Remember the quote, "you are stronger than you think"? Well, you are stronger than you think because what you think (thoughts) are not facts.

How often would you say your thoughts (that voice) has talked you out of doing things? ☐

I DON'T WANT TO FEEL ANXIOUS ANYMORE

I woke to the same sense of despair that would squash any hope of ever recovering each morning.

Repeatedly I was advised to stop resisting the anxiety and learn to accept it instead, but I didn't want to because my biggest fear was that if I stopped, I'd become lost in anxiety forever. Ten years later, I was still resisting, avoiding and white-knuckling my way through life. Something had to change, and that was my approach.

It's so easy to fall into the cycle where you desperately want to overcome anxiety, yet you fear it too much to change how you react and move forward when you don't have all the facts. Dr Claire Weekes gave me those facts, explaining what was happening to me and how to recover, and more importantly, showed me how my current daily behaviours kept me stuck.

I didn't want to feel anxious anymore, so I had no other choice than to change how I responded to it.

Making changes felt scary but shifting the behaviours that fuelled my anxiety was necessary. THE PAIN WAS SHORT-LIVED when I stopped resisting and felt much more manageable because I knew it would lead to my recovery. It takes time, but you begin to feel more empowered every day.

Realising that you're experiencing prolonged anxiety because you are doing the things that fuel it is a proper eye-opener, and it is hard to unsee once seen. So, I went from continuously falling down the rabbit hole to asking myself, 'will this fuel or weaken the anxiety?' and if it fuelled it, it was no longer an option for me.

What scares you the most about changing how you approach anxiety? ☐

IT'S NEVER AS BAD AS WE THINK

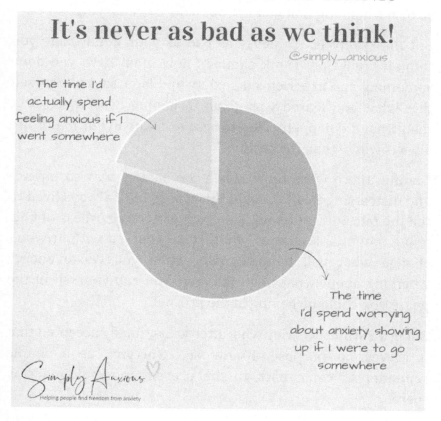

How often have you experienced this, where you've worried yourself sick about doing something in case you become anxious only to find that once there, the anxiety subsides pretty quickly?

It's a typical occurrence for those who have developed a fear of anxiety. The very thought of having a panic attack or high anxiety away from home, in public and becoming stuck can be so overwhelming that you opt out before even trying.

But the reality is, it's never as bad as your mind made you think it would be. Think about it: how often have you done something and experienced anxiety and later said to yourself that what you feared was going to happen was way worse than what did happen? The stories we create in our minds are always worse than the reality.

I admit, there were times when the anxiety was so intense and distressing that I thought this was it, but I always lived to tell the tale and got home. The truth is that regardless of how many potential scenarios you torture yourself with, it won't change what will happen. Also, when you waste energy worrying about what might happen, you rob yourself of the peace you could be having in the present.

Being a chronic worrier who, after years, finally accepted that it serves no purpose, I now see worrying as a simple reminder to come back to the present moment and stay there!

If you find yourself worrying, stop and shift your attention to imagining all the fantastic possibilities that can happen if you just let go of the worry and start trusting in yourself and embracing uncertainty.

YOU CAN'T WAIT UNTIL LIFE ISN'T HARD – NIGHTBIRDE

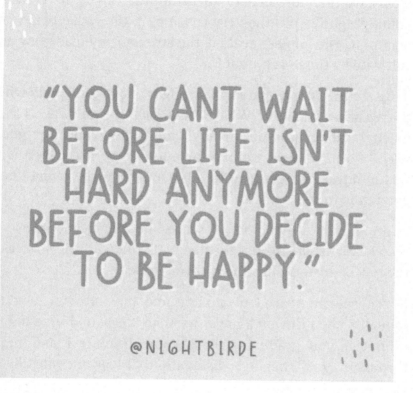

"YOU CANT WAIT BEFORE LIFE ISN'T HARD ANYMORE BEFORE YOU DECIDE TO BE HAPPY."

@NIGHTBIRDE

I would wait for the best time to face my fears because I'd always question, if harmless, why does anxiety feel so scary and debilitating?

The answer was always the same - it's supposed to. It's a threat response, and its sole purpose is to grab your attention and move you out of harm's way. If it weren't so alarming, it wouldn't work, and you'd walk right into the path of danger. When a genuine threat triggers anxiety, it can save your life.

I was waiting for anxiety to disappear all by itself while holding tightly onto the very cause of it, the cause being 'my fear' of it. The longer I waited, the stronger my fear grew and cultivated a ton of self-doubt.

'I'll go to the shop when I feel stronger; I'll go for a walk when the weather's better.' What I was saying here was, 'I'll go when I can guarantee anxiety won't show up.' But guess what? I'd have been waiting for a long time if I stayed with this mindset because that mindset never made it feel like a good time to try.

Waiting is like avoiding; it serves no positive purpose in recovery. Instead, it just further fuels the fear and increases the risk of anxiety showing up even more.

If you remain scared of anxiety and buy into the anxious thoughts about it, you'll never feel like it's a good time to face it. But if you gradually allow yourself to feel and move through it, you'll begin to dismantle that fear and start living the life you want to. ☐

THERE ARE MORE THINGS THAT FRIGHTEN US IN OUR IMAGINATION

"THERE ARE MORE THINGS THAT FRIGHTEN US THAN INJURE US, AND WE SUFFER MORE IN IMAGINATION THAN REALITY."

@SIMPLY_ANXIOUS

This SOIC quote is spot on! I have been frightened more by my anxious thoughts/predictions than I have by anything I've experienced in life.

Yes, I have had some challenging times, don't get me wrong, but any fear or terror has always been from my thoughts. Thoughts can create whatever they want and describe the worst-case scenario and outcome to even the simplest of things. They can turn a molehill into a mountain, and if we believe them, we suffer as if what they are saying is 100% going to happen.

Learning not to take your thoughts so seriously takes practice, catching yourself before you slide right down that rabbit hole by asking yourself, 'Is this true? Where is the evidence?'

It's also helpful to accept that you'll never get to a stage where the mind doesn't produce scary thoughts because that's just how the mind works. But you will get to a place where you no longer become entangled in the stories and cause yourself unnecessary suffering. Learning not to give these thoughts your attention allows them to come and go without you noticing them so much.

Remember, if what you're thinking is not happening right now in reality, it doesn't deserve your attention. And trusting the thoughts that tell you about what the future holds is pointless because the mind cannot predict the future.

You can't control your thoughts, but you can control how to react to them☐

CHAPTER TWELVE

Resources That Helped with My Recovery

I wanted to share some of the resources that helped me during my recovery. Remember that what works for one person may not work for another, so please don't consider it your fault if something doesn't work or feel right for you. Please also remember that although patience, consistency, and repetition are essential for recovery, so is self-care.

Books that helped with my recovery and beyond *(I have read so many books throughout my anxiety journey, but these are the ones that helped me the most and some of which I still use today.)*

DR CLAIRE WEEKES

- *Self Help for Your Nerves* (1962)

- *Simple, Effective Treatment of Agoraphobia* (1976)

- *More Help for Your Nerves* (1984)

- *The Latest Help for Your Nerves* (1989)

My absolute 'go-to' for understanding anxiety and guiding me through exposure therapy. This lady's words saved my life, and I will be forever grateful for her work.

PAUL DAVID

At Last, a Life: Anxiety and Panic Free (2006)

This awesome book not only inspired me, it gave me comfort from seeing how a fellow sufferer recovered.

MICHAEL SINGER

The Untethered Soul: The Journey Beyond Yourself (2007)

This book is genius and for me opened a whole new way of looking at emotional wellbeing and the mind. Each time I read this book I learn something new.

ECKHART TOLLE

The Power of Now: A Guide to Spiritual Enlightenment (1997)

This amazing book completely changed my outlook on life and the way I choose to see it/live it: once changed, you can't go back.

BRESSEL VAN DER KOLK

The Body Keeps the Score: Brain, Mind, and Body in the Healing of Trauma (2014)

This book was so helpful for me to understand trauma and how I could work through my own experience. Be mindful that there are real-life case studies in the book so it could be triggering. But for me it really gave me the deep understanding I needed.

MATT HAIG

Notes on a Nervous Planet (2018)

I love this book: no nonsense with some good humour. Really helpful for me to dip in and out of and I think everyone with anxiety would benefit from reading.

EMMY BRUNNER

Find your True Voice: Stop Listening to Your Inner Critic, Heal Your Trauma and Live a Life Full of Joy (2021)

I recommend this book to everyone. I read it after I had recovered from my anxiety disorder but while working through my other emotional stuff! It is such a kind and soothing book; it made me feel safe and like the author was talking directly to me.

PODCASTS that help to educate, inspire, and keep me healthy *(I know podcasts are not for everyone, but I just love listening to them while driving or out on a walk. The ones I* *have listed I've found inspirational and motivating which is what I believe we all need in life. Less drama and more inspiration.)*

Happy Place – Fearne Cotton

Must be my favourite of all. It's like food for the soul. Fearne is definitely leading the way for emotional, mental health, and wellbeing awareness (certainly within the UK) and is also a great source of support in my opinion. Her podcast is full of amazing tips and those golden nuggets we all search for to make sense of what we go through as humans. I can't get enough of this podcast and the variety of guests is awesome.

Slo Mo – Mo Gawdat

Mo Gawdat and some of his wisest friends explore the profound questions and obstacles we all face.

The Waffle Shop – Taylor James

I adore this podcast because it is hosted by someone I personally find totally inspirational (you need to hear his story as to why). James is a natural at hosting which makes it a pleasant and easy listen. He talks about topics with his guests that really do need more light shined upon. This podcast is funny at times, hugely insightful, and genius.

The Diary of a CEO – Steven Bartlett

I adore everything that comes out of Steven Bartlett's mouth, but I have to say I was a little reluctant to try his podcast because I thought it might just be about business. I was completely wrong and it has become one of my absolute favourites. His outlook and perspective on life shines out in every episode. The topics cover everything including mental health and wellbeing. I have personally had so much inspiration and comfort from listening.

Supplements that help with my anxiety and overall wellbeing *(Always check with your GP before taking any supplements.)*

I don't believe that supplements can cure an anxiety disorder but having the right amount of nutrients daily I believe can support recovery and help with your overall wellbeing. The ones listed below are those that have made a personal difference to anxiety recovery.

Magnesium glycinate

The best type of magnesium to take because it may help with brain functions that reduce anxiety and stress, as well as regulating blood sugar levels. I still take these daily.

Vitamin B complex

Group of eight nutrients that work together to support and manage processes in the body including stress and mood stabilisation.

Vitamin D

Plays an important role in mood regulation as well as nerve and brain health.

Omega-3 oil

Because the body can't produce these fats we rely on our diet to provide them. Some studies suggest Omega-3 supplements can help reduce anxiety symptoms.

I also take a daily probiotic for my gut health.

Exercise that helped with my recovery and continues to help with my mental wellbeing

Walking

It got me out of the house and into nature which always had a calming effect on me. I began practising mindfulness on my walks or used the time to listen to audiobooks by qualified authors like Dr Weekes, or inspiring podcasts.

Kundalini yoga

This type of yoga uses the breath as well as poses and mantras. It is said to relieve stress and anxiety and improves cognitive function which is exactly what I found when I started attending sessions. This yoga has helped me heal my periods of GAD and has helped me to focus and calm my mind when it's busy. I absolutely love it and think it should be on prescription for everyone suffering with stress-related illness.

Wild water swimming

I am relatively new to this and only started after I'd recovered from anxiety. But it is something I can see myself continuing because each time I have been it has given me such a powerful grounding and healing effect. It boosts dopamine and serotonin levels and stimulates the release of feel-good endorphins. Most people I have met doing these swims are all doing so to heal their mental health. Remember safety must come first when considering swimming outdoors, so my only advice would be to join a group who run wild water swimming meetups professionally.

If you would like to hear more from me,
please follow me on Instagram @simply_anxious

NOTES

_____

_____

_____

_____

_____

_____

_____

_____

_____

_____

_____

_____

_____

_____

_____

_____

Printed in Great Britain
by Amazon